THE GOURMET'S
GUIDE TO EUROPE

The pleasures of the table are common to all ages and ranks, to all countries and times; they not only harmonise with all the other pleasures, but remain to console us for their loss.

BRILLAT SAVARIN.

PREFACE

Often enough, staying in a hotel in a foreign town, I have wished to sally forth and to dine or breakfast at the typical restaurant of the place, should there be one. Almost invariably I have found great difficulty in obtaining any information regarding any such restaurant. The proprietor of the caravanserai at which one is staying may admit vaguely that there are eating-houses in the town, but asks why one should be anxious to seek for second-class establishments when the best restaurant in the country is to be found under his roof. The hall-porter has even less scruples, and stigmatises every feeding-place outside the hotel as a den of thieves, where the stranger foolishly venturing is certain to be poisoned and then robbed. This book is an attempt to help the man who finds himself in such a position. His guide-book may possibly give him the names of the restaurants, but it does no more. My co-author and myself attempt to give him some details—what his surroundings will be, what dishes are the specialities of the house, what wine a wise man will order, and what bill he is likely to be asked to pay.

Our ambition was to deal fully with the capitals of all the countries of Europe, the great seaports, the pleasure resorts, and the "show places." The most acute critic will not be more fully aware how far we have fallen short of our ideal than we are, and no critic can have any idea of the difficulty of making such a book as we hope this will some day be when complete. At all events we have always gone to the best authorities where we had not the knowledge ourselves. Our publisher, Mr. Grant Richards, quite entered into the idea that no advertisements of any kind from hotels or restaurants should be allowed within the covers of the book; and though we have asked for information from all classes of gourmets—from ambassadors to the simple globe-trotter—we have not listened to any man interested directly or indirectly in any hotel or restaurant.

Hotels as places to live in we have not considered critically, and have only mentioned them when the restaurants attached to them are the dining-places patronised by the *bon-vivants* of the town.

Over England we have not thrown our net, for *Dinners and Diners* leaves me nothing new to write of London restaurants.

In conclusion I beg, on behalf of my co-author and myself, to return thanks to all the good fellows who have given us information; and I would earnestly beg any travelling gourmet, who finds any change in the restaurants we have mentioned, or who comes on treasure-trove in the shape of some delightful dining-place we know nothing of, to take pen and ink and write word of it to me, his humble servant, to the care of Mr. Grant Richards, Leicester Square. So shall he benefit, in future editions, all his own kind. We hear much of the kindness of the poor to the poor. This is an opportunity, if not for the rich to be kind to the rich, at least for those who deserve to be rich to benefit their fellows.

N. NEWNHAM-DAVIS.

CONTENTS

CHAPTER I—PARIS 15
 The "Cuisine de Paris"—A little ancient history—Restaurants with a "past"—The restaurants of today—Over the river—Open-air restaurants—Supping-places—Miscellaneous.

CHAPTER II—FRENCH PROVINCIAL TOWNS 41
 The northern ports—Norman and Breton towns—The west coast and Bordeaux—Marseilles and the Riviera—The Pyrenees—Provence—Aix-les-Bains and other "cure" places.

CHAPTER III—BELGIAN TOWNS 75
 The food of the country—Antwerp—Spa—Bruges—Ostende.

CHAPTER IV—BRUSSELS 84
 The Savoy—The Epaule de Mouton—The Faille Déchirée—The Lion d'Or—The Regina—The Helder—The Filet de Sole—Wiltcher's—Justine's—The Etoile—The Belveder—The Café Riche—Duranton's—The Laiterie—Miscellaneous.

CHAPTER V—HOLLAND 95
 Restaurants at the Hague—Amsterdam—Scheveningen—Rotterdam—The food of the people.

CHAPTER VI—GERMAN TOWNS 100
   The cookery of the country—Rathskeller and beer-cellars—Dresden—München—Nüremburg—Hanover—Leipsic—Frankfurt—Düsseldorf—The Rhine valley—"Cure" places—Kiel—Hamburg.

CHAPTER VII—BERLIN 126
   Up-to-date restaurants—Supping-places—Military cafés—Night restaurants.

CHAPTER VIII—SWITZERLAND 132
   Lucerne—Basle—Bern—Geneva—Davos Platz.

CHAPTER IX—ITALY 137
   Italian cookery and wines—Turin—Milan—Genoa—Venice—Bologna—Spezzia—Florence—Pisa—Leghorn—Rome—Naples—Palermo.

CHAPTER X—SPAIN AND PORTUGAL 152
   Food and wines of the country—Barcelona—San Sebastian—Bilbao—Madrid—Seville—Bobadilla—Grenada—Jerez—Algeciras—Lisbon—Estoril.

CHAPTER XI—AUSTRIA AND HUNGARY 167
   Viennese restaurants and cafés—Baden—Carlsbad—Marienbad—Prague—Bad Gastein—Budapesth.

CHAPTER XII—ROUMANIA 175
   The dishes of the country—The restaurants of Bucarest.

CHAPTER XIII—SWEDEN. NORWAY. DENMARK 178
   Stockholm restaurants—Malmö—Storvik—Gothenburg—Christiana—Copenhagen—Elsinore.

CHAPTER XIV—RUSSIA 184
　　Food of the country—Restaurants in Moscow—The dining places of St. Petersburg—Odessa—Warsaw.

CHAPTER XV—TURKEY 191
　　Turkish dishes—Constantinople restaurants.

CHAPTER XVI—GREECE 195
　　Grecian Dishes—Athens.

CHAPTER I

PARIS

The "Cuisine de Paris"—A little ancient history—Restaurants with a "past"—The restaurants of today—Over the river—Open-air restaurants—Supping-places—Miscellaneous.

Paris is the culinary centre of the world. All the great missionaries of good cookery have gone forth from it, and its cuisine was, is, and ever will be the supreme expression of one of the greatest arts in the world. Most of the good cooks come from the south of France, most of the good food comes from the north. They meet at Paris, and thus the Paris cuisine, which is that of the nation and that of the civilised world, is created.

When the Channel has been crossed you are in the country of good soups, of good fowl, of good vegetables, of good sweets, of good wine. The *hors-d'œuvre* are a Russian innovation; but since the days when Henry IV. vowed that every peasant should have a fowl in his pot, soup from the simplest *bouillon* to the most lordly *consommés* and splendid *bisques* has been better made in France than anywhere else in the world. Every great cook of France has invented some particularly delicate variety of the boiled fillet of sole, and Dugleré achieved a place amongst the immortals, by his manipulation of the brill. The soles of the north are as good as any that ever came out of British waters; and Paris—sending tentacles west to the waters where the sardines swim, and south to the home of the lamprey, and tapping a thousand streams for trout and the tiny gudgeon and crayfish—can show as noble a list of fishes as any city in the world. The *chef de cuisine* who could not enumerate an hundred and fifty entrées all distinctively French, would be no proficient in his noble profession. The British beef stands against all the world as the meat noblest for the spit, though the French ox which has worked its time in the fields gives the best material for the soup-pot; and though the Welsh lamb and the English sheep are the perfection of mutton young and mutton old, the lamb nurtured on milk till the hour of its death, and the sheep reared on the salt-marshes of the north, make splendid contribution to the Paris kitchens. Veal is practically an unknown meat in London; and the calf which has been fed on milk and yolk of egg, and which has flesh as soft as a kiss and as white as snow, is only to be found in the Parisian restaurants. Most of the good restaurants in London import all their winged creatures, except game, from France; and the Surrey fowl and the Aylesbury duck, the representatives of Great Britain, make no great show against the champions of Gaul, though the Norfolk turkey holds his own. A vegetable dish, served by itself and not flung into the gravy of a joint, forms part of every French dinner, large or small; and in the battle of the kitchen gardens the foreigners beat us nearly all along the line, though I think that English asparagus is better than the white monsters of Argenteuil. A truffled partridge, or the homely *Perdrix au choux*, or the splendid *Faisan à la Financière* show that there are many more ways of treating a game bird than plain roasting him; and the peasants of the south of France had crushed the bones of their ducks for a century before we in London ever heard of *Canard à la Presse*. The Parisian eats a score of little birds we are too proud to mention in our cookery books, and he knows the difference between a *mauviette* and an *alouette*. Perhaps the greatest abasement of the Briton, whose ancestors called the French "Froggies" in scorn, comes when his first morning in Paris he orders for breakfast with joyful expectation a dish of the thighs of the little frogs from the vineyards. An Austrian pastry-cook has a lighter hand than a

French one, but the Parisian open tarts and cakes and the *friandises* and the ice, or *coupe-jacque* at the end of the Gallic repast are excellent.

Paris is strewn with the wrecks of restaurants, and many of the establishments with great names of our grandfathers' and fathers' days are now only *tavernes* or cheap *table-d'hôte* restaurants. The Grand Vefour in the Palais Royal—where the patrons of the establishment in Louis Philippe's time used to eat off royal crockery, bought from the surplus stock of the palaces by M. Hamel, cook to the king, and proprietor of the restaurant—has lost its vogue in the world of fashion. The present Café de Paris has an excellent cook, and is the supper restaurant where the most shimmering lights of the *demi-monde* may be seen; but the old Café de Paris, at the corner of the Rue Taitbout, the house which M. Martin Guépet brought to such fame, and where the *Veau à la Casserole* drew the warmest praise from our grandfathers, has vanished. Bignon's, which was a name known throughout the world, has fallen from its high estate; the Café Riche, though it retains a good restaurant, is not the old famous dining-place any longer; and the Marivaux, where Joseph flourished, has been transformed into a *brasserie*. The Café Hardi, at one time a very celebrated restaurant, made place for the Maison d'Or, and the gilded glory of the latter has now passed in its turn. The Café Veron, Philippe's, of the Rue Mont Orgueil, and the Rocher de Cancale in the Rue Mandar, where Borel, one of the cooks of Napoleon I., made gastronomic history, Beauvilliers's, the proprietor of which was a friend of all the field-marshals of Europe, and made and lost half-a-dozen fortunes, the Trois Frères Provençeaux, the Café Very, and D'Hortesio's are but memories.

The saddest disappearance of all, because the latest, is the Maison d'Or, which is to be converted, so it is said, into a *brasserie*. The retirement of Casimir, one of the Verdier family, who was to the D'Or what Dugleré was to the Anglais, precipitated the catastrophe, and in the autumn of 1902 the house gave its farewell luncheon, and closed with all the honours of war. Alas for the *Carpe à la Gelée* and the *Sole au vin Rouge* and the *Poularde*

Maison d'Or! I shall never, I fear, eat their like again. There was much history attached to the little golden house; more, perhaps, than to any other restaurant in the world. From its doors Rigolboche, in the costume of Mother Eve, started for her run across the road to the Anglais. At the table by one of the windows looking out on to the boulevard Nestor Roqueplan, Fould, Salamanca, and Delahante used always to dine. Upstairs in "Le Grand 6," which was to the Maison d'Or what "Le Grand 16" is to the Anglais, Salamanca, who drew a vast revenue from a Spanish banking-house, used to give extraordinary suppers at which the lights of the *demi-monde* of that day, Cora Pearl, Anna Deslions, Deveria, and others used to be present. The amusement of the Spaniard used to be to spill the wax from a candle over the dresses, and then to pay royally for the damage. One evening he asked one of the MM. Verdier whether a very big bill would be presented to him if he burned the whole house down, and on being told that it was only a matter of two or three million francs he would have set light to the curtains if M. Verdier had not interfered to prevent him. The "beau Demidoff," the duelling Baron Espeleta, Princes Galitzin and Murat, Tolstoy, and the Duc de Rivoli gave their parties in the "Grand 6"; and down the narrow, steep flight of steps which led into the side street the Duke of Hamilton fell and broke his neck. The Maison d'Or was the meeting-place, in the sixty odd years of its existence, of many celebrities of literature. Dumas, Meilhac, Emmanuel Arène used to dine there before they went across the road for a game of cards at the Cercle des Deux Mondes, and later Oncle Sarcey was one of the *habitués* of the house.

Two restaurants in particular seem to me to head the list of the classic, quiet establishments, proud of having a long history, satisfied with their usual *clientèle*, non-advertising, content to rest on their laurels. Those two are the Anglais and Voisin's, the former on the Boulevard des Italiens, the latter in the Rue St-Honoré. The Café Anglais, the white-faced house at the corner of the Rue Marivaux, is the senior of the two, for it has a history of more than a hundred years. It was originally a little wine-merchant's shop, with its door leading into the Rue Marivaux, and was owned by a M. Chevereuil. The ownerships of MM. Chellet and de L'Homme marked successive steps in its upward career, and when the restaurant came into the market in '79 or '80 it was bought by a syndicate of bankers and other rich business men who parted with it to its present proprietor. The Comte de Grammont Caderousse and his companions in what used to be known as the "Loge Infernale" at the old Opera, were the best-known patrons of the Anglais; and until the Opera House, replaced by the present building, was burnt down, the Anglais was a great supping-place, the little rabbit-hutches of the *entresol* being the scene of some of the wildest and most interesting parties given by the great men of the Second Empire. The history of the Anglais has never been written because, as the proprietor will tell you, it never *could* be written without telling tales anent great men which should not be put into print; but if you ask to see the book of menus, chiefly of dinners given in the "Grand Seize," the room on the first floor, the curve of the windows of which look up the long line of the boulevards, and if you are shown the treasure you will find in it records of dinners given by King Edward when he was Prince of Wales, by the Duc de Morny and by D'Orsay, by all the Grand Dukes who ever came out of Russia, by "Citron" and Le Roi Milan, by the lights of the French jockey club, and many other celebrities. There is one especially interesting menu of a dinner at which Bismarck was a guest—before the terrible year of course. While I am gossiping as to the curiosities of the Anglais I must not forget a little collection of glass and silver in a cabinet in the passage of the *entresol*. Every piece has a history, and most of them have had royal owners. The great sight of the restaurant, however, is its cellars. Electric light is used to light them, luminous grapes hang from the arches, and an orange tree at the end of a vista glows with transparent fruit. In these cellars, beside the wine on the wine-list of the restaurant, are to be found some bottles of all the great vintage years of claret, an object-lesson in Bordeaux; and there are little stores of brandies of wondrous age, most of which were already in the cellars when the battle of Waterloo was fought.

From a gourmet's point of view the great interest in the restaurant will lie, if he wishes to give a large dinner, in the Grand Seize or one of the other private rooms; if he is going to dine alone, or is going to take his wife out to dinner, in the triangular room on the ground floor with its curtains of lace, its white walls, its mirrors and its little gilt tripod in the centre of the floor. Dugleré was the *chef* who, above all others, made history at the Anglais, and the present proprietor, M. Burdel, was one of his pupils; and therefore the cookery of Dugleré is the cookery still of the Anglais. *Potage Germiny* is claimed by the Café Anglais as a dish invented by the house, but the Maison d'Or across the way also laid claim to it, and told an anecdote of its creation—how it was invented by Casimir for the Marquis de St-George. The various fish *à la Dugleré* there can be no question concerning, the *Barbue Dugleré* being the most celebrated; and the *Poularde Albufera* and the *Filet de Sole Mornay* (which was also claimed by the Grand Vefour) are both specialities of the house. You can order as expensive a dinner as you will for a great feast at the Anglais, and you can eat rich dishes if you desire it; but there is no reason that you should not dine there very well, and as cheaply as you can expect to get good material, good cooking, and good attendance anywhere in the world. The "dishes of the day" are always excellent, and I have dined off a plate of soup, a pint of Bordeaux, and some slices of a *gigot de sept heures*—one of the greatest achievements of cookery—for a very few francs. I always find that I can dine amply, and on food that even a German doctor could not object to, for less than a louis. For instance, a dinner at the Anglais of half-a-dozen Ostende Oysters, *Potage Laitues et Quenelles*, *Merlans Frits*, *Cuisse de Poularde de Rôtie*, *Salade Romaine*, cheese, half a bottle of Graves 1e Cru, and a bottle of St-Galmier costs 18 francs.

Voisin's, in the Rue St-Honoré, the corner house whose windows, curtained with lace, promise dignified quiet, is a restaurant which has a history, and has, and has had, great names amongst its *habitués*. Many of these have been diplomats, and Voisin's knows that ambassadors do not care to have their doings, when free from the cares of office, gossiped about. When I first saw Voisin's, it looked as unlike the house of today as can be imagined. I was in Paris immediately after the days of the Commune and followed, with an old General, the line the troops had taken in the fight for the city. In the Rue St-Honoré were some of the fiercest combats, for the regulars fought their way from house to house down this street to turn the positions the Communists took up in the Champs Elysées and the gardens of the Tuileries. The British Embassy had become a hospital, and all the houses which had not been burned looked as though they had stood a bombardment. There were bullet splashes on all the walls, and I remember that Voisin's looked even more battered and hopeless than did most of its neighbours.

The diplomats have always had an affection for Voisin's, perhaps because of its nearness to the street of the Embassies; and in the "eighties" the attachés of the British Embassy used to breakfast there every day. Nowadays, the *clientèle* seems to me to be a mixture of the best type of the English and Americans passing through Paris, and the more elderly amongst the statesmen, who were no doubt the dashing young blades of twenty-five years ago. The two comfortable ladies who sit near the door at the desk, and the little show-table of the finest fruit seem to me never to have changed, and there is still the same quiet-footed, unhurrying service which impressed me when first I made the acquaintance of the restaurant. It is one of the dining-places where one feels that to dine well and unhurriedly is the first great business of life, and that everything else must wait at the dinner-hour. The proprietor, grey-headed and distinguished-looking, goes from table to table saying a word or two to the *habitués*, and there is a sense of peace in the place—a reflection of the sunshine and calm of Provence, whence the founder of the restaurant came.

The great glory of Voisin's is its cellar of red wines, its Burgundies and Bordeaux. The Bordeaux are arranged in their proper precedence, the wines from the great vineyards first, and the rest in their correct order down to mere bourgeois tipple. Against each brand is the price of the vintage of all the years within a drinkable period, and the man who knew the wine-list of Voisin's thoroughly would be the greatest authority in the world on claret.

Mr. Rowland Strong, in his book on Paris, tells how, one Christmas Eve, he took an Englishman to dine at Voisin's, and how that Englishman demanded plum-pudding. The *maître-d'hôtel* was equal to the occasion. He was polite but firm, and his assertion that "The House of Voisin does not serve, has never served, and will never serve, plum-pudding" settled the matter.

If the Anglais and Voisin's may be said to have much of their interest in their "past," Paillard's should be taken as a restaurant which is the type and parent of the present up-to-date restaurant. The white restaurant on the Boulevard des Italiens has kept at the top of the tree for many years, and has sent out more culinary missionaries to improve the taste of dining man than any other establishment in Paris. Joseph, who brought the Marivaux to such a high pitch of fame before he emigrated to London, came from Paillard's and so did Frederic of the Tour d'Argent, of whom I shall have something to say later on. Henri of the Gaillon, Notta, Charles of Foyot's—all were trained at Paillard's.

The restaurant has its history, and its long list of great patrons. *Le Désir de Roi*, which generally appears in the menu of any important dinner at Paillard's, and which has *foie gras* as its principal component, has been eaten by a score of kings at one time or another, our own gracious Majesty heading the list. The restaurant at first was contained in one small room. Then the shop of Isabelle, the Jockey Club flower-girl, which was next door, was acquired, and lastly another little shop was taken in, the entrance changed from the front to its present position at the side, the accountant's desk put out of sight, and the little musicians' gallery built—for Paillard's has moved with the time and now has a band of Tziganes, much to the grief of men like myself who prefer conversation to music as the accompaniment of a meal. The restaurant as it is with its white walls and bas-reliefs of cupids and flowers, its green Travertine panels let into the white pilasters, its chandeliers of cut glass, is very handsome. M. Paillard, hair parted in the middle and with a small moustache, irreproachably attired, wearing a grey frock-coat by day, and a "smoking" and black tie in the evening, is generally to be seen superintending all arrangements, and there is a *maître-d'hôtel* who speaks excellent English, and a head waiter with whiskers who deserted to Henri, but subsequently returned, who is also an accomplished linguist.

Amongst the specialities of the house are *Pomme Otero* and *Pomme Georgette*, both created, I fancy, by Joseph when he was at Paillard's, *Homard Cardinal, Filet de Sole à la Russe, Sole Paillard, Filet de Sole Kotchoubey, Timbale de queues d'Ecrevisses Mantua, Côte de Bœuf braisé Empire, Pommes Macaire, Filet Paillard, Suprême de Volaille Grand Duc, Rouennais Paillard, Baron d'agneau Henri IV., Poularde Archiduc, Poularde à la Derby, Poularde Wladimir, Filet de Selle Czarine, Bécasse au Fumet, Rouennais à la Presse, Terrine de Foie Gras à la gelée au Porto, Perdreau et Caille Paillard*.

Two menus of dinners M. Paillard has given me, one a very noble feast, to the length of which I am a conscientious objector but which I print, presently, in full, and the other a banquet of lesser grandeur with *Crème Germiny, Barbue Paillard, Ortolans en surprise, Salade Idéale*, and many other good things in it from which I select the following dishes as making a typical little Paillard feast for two, the price of which would not be a king's ransom:—

Caviar frais.
Consommé Viveur.
Filets de Sole Joinville.
Cœurs de Filet Rachel.
Pommes Anna.
Haricots Verts à la Touranquelle.
An Ice or some iced Fruits and some Coffee.

And this repast might well be washed down by a bottle of Montrachet 1885, with a glass of Fine Champagne Palais de St-Cloud to follow.

This is the menu of the banquet:—

Le Caviar Impérial.
Les Huîtres de Burnham.
Le Consommé Paillard.
Pailles Parmesan.
La Crème d'Arétin.
Les Croustades à la Victoria.
La Carpe à la Chambord.
Le Turbot à l'Amiral.
Le Baron de Pauillac persillé.
Les pommes Macaire.
Le Velouté Favorite.
Le Désir de Roi.
Les Bécasses au fumet.
La Salade Espérance.
Les Asperges d'Argenteuil S^{ce} Mousseline.
La Pyramide à l'Ananas.
Le Soufflé aux Mandarines.
Macarons et Gaufrettes Chantilly.
La Corbeille de Fruits.
Café.

Eau-de-vie Russe.
Chablis Moutonne.
Johannisberg 1893.

Mouton Rothschild 1875.

Clos Vougeot 1858.
Moët brut 1884.
Fine Champagne des Tuileries 1800.

What the cost of this feast would be it is difficult to estimate, and I will not even hazard a guess.

I asked, last spring, an Englishman who knows his Paris better than most Parisians, what he would consider a typical breakfast, dinner, and supper in Paris, and he answered, "Breakfast *chez Henri* at the Gaillon, dine at the Ritz, and sup at Durand's."

There are two Henri's in Paris, one is the little hotel and English bar, and the other is in the Place Gaillon. Henri's Restaurant Gaillon had its days of celebrity in the Second Empire, and then sank, as the Maison Grossetête, from grace until Henri Drouet, leaving Paillard's, established himself there. When I first knew the restaurant it had Paillard's cookery, but not Paillard's prices; but now that the whole of the *monde qui dîne* has found it out, I fancy that the scale of prices has risen to a level with that of the parent restaurant. The first room is the best one to breakfast or dine in, for the others on hot days are apt to be very stuffy; and it is well to order a table by telephone in advance. Henri's, it always seems to me, has a more tempting table of cold viands, patés, and tarts and *friandises* set out than any other restaurateur's, and many of the *habitués* at lunch-time order eggs or fish, and then turn their attention to the cold buffet.

When dining at Henri's the *Consommé Fortunato*, the *filets de sole* of the restaurant, the *Noisettes de Veau Port Mahon*, the *Crêpes des Gourmets* should be remembered. If you want a dinner for twelve, you cannot do better than order the following, or rather select dishes from it, for it is unreasonably lengthy as it stands:—

Hors-d'œuvre à la Russe.

POTAGES.

Consommé Viveur.
Pailles et Parmesan.

POISSON.

Timbale de Homard à l'Américaine.

ENTRÉES.

Baron de Pauillac à la Boulangère.
Endives Pochées au jus.
Escalopes de Foies grand Opéra.

Rôti.

Bécasses Flambées au fumet.
Salade Port Mahon.
Mousse Bohémienne glacée.
Truffes au Champagne à la gelée.

Légumes.

Asperges fraîches. S^{ce} Mousseline.

Entremets.

Soufflé Valenciennes.
Poires Gaillon.

There are several other restaurants which claim to be quite first class, and which are smart and amusing. Two such are the restaurants facing the Madeleine, Durand's, and La Rue's. It was in one of the little rooms on the first floor of Durand's that the Brav' General sat debating in his mind whether he should initiate a *coup d'état*, and the crowd outside waited and watched, expecting something to happen. Nothing did happen. General Boulanger thought so long, that the decisive moment passed, and he went home to bed. Boulanger has gone, but his friends, grey-headed now, breakfast daily at Durand's. La Rue's was also a restaurant in favour with General Boulanger, and I fancy that the little dinner-parties he gave there helped much to bring the place into celebrity. Both these restaurants have lately been enlarged and redecorated, and La Rue's advertises a great deal, which no doubt has increased its *clientèle*, but which has not decreased its prices. Parisian Society has decreed that it is "smart" to sup at Durand's, and I always find it an excellent place at which to breakfast. The last time that I took my morning meal there I found all the younger members of the British Embassy breakfasting there, a sure sign that the place is just now on the crest of the wave.

Some of the specialities of Durand's are *Potage Henri IV.*, *Consommé Baigneuse*, *petits diables*, *Barbue Durand*, *Poulet Sauté Grand Duc*, *Salade Georgette*, *Soufflé Pôle Nord*, and of course a variation of the inevitable *canard à la presse* and the woodcock subjected to an *auto-da-fé*.

This is the supper that the Restaurant Durand gave its clients on the greatest supping night of the year, Christmas Eve, 1902. The *boudin* of course all Paris has for supper on the night before the great Christmas feast:—

>Consommé de Volaille au fumet de Céleris.
>Boudin grillé à la Parisienne.
>Ailerons de Volaille à la Tzar.
>Cailles à la Lucullus.
>Salade Durand.
>Ecrevisses de la Meuse à la nage.
>Crêpes Suzette.
>Dessert.
>Champagnes.
>Clicquot Brut, Pommery Drapeau Américain.
>Gde Fine Napoléon.

At La Rue's I have felt inclined sometimes to protest when I have been charged 2 francs for half-a-dozen prawns, and to think that the vermillion-coloured seats are being paid for too quickly out of profits; but I rarely pass through Paris without breakfasting there, and eating the cold poached eggs in jelly, the *Grenouilles à la Marinière*, or one of the dishes of cold fish which are excellently served. Some of the specialities of the house are *Potage Reine, Barbue à la Russe, Caille à la Souvaroff, Tournedos à la Rossini, Caneton de Rouen au Sang, Bécasse Flambée, Salade Gauloise, Crêpes Suzette, Glace Gismonda, Pêches Flambées* and from this list any one could choose either a little dinner or a big one.

Of restaurants attached to hotels I do not propose to write in this article, with one exception, for there are few of the hundreds of hotels at which one cannot get a very fair dinner; and at some, such as the Elysée Palace, over which Caesario presides, one can get an excellent one; but the purpose of this book is to give information to the man who wishes to dine away from hotels. The one exception is the Ritz, in the Place Vendôme, and I include this in my list because the Ritz is a restaurant firstly, and an hotel secondly, and because as a dining place it holds an exceptional position in Paris. It is the restaurant of the smartest foreign society in Paris, and the English, Americans, Russians, Spaniards, dining there always outnumber greatly the French. It is a place of great feasts, but it is also a restaurant at which the *maîtres-d'hôtel* are instructed not to suggest long dinners to the patrons of the establishment. In M. Elles' hands or that of the *maître-d'hôtel* there is no fear of being "rushed" into ordering an over-lengthy repast. This is a typical little dinner for three I once ate at the Ritz, and as a feast in the autumn it is worth recording and repeating:—

Caviar.
Consommé Viveni.
Mousseline de Soles au vin du Rhin.
Queues d'Ecrevisses à l'Américaine.
Escalopes de Riz de veau Favorite.
Perdreaux Truffés.
Salade.
Asperges vertes en branches.
Coupes aux Marrons.
Friandises.

In the afternoon the long passage with its chairs, carpets, and hangings all of crushed strawberry colour is filled with tea-drinkers, for the "5 o'clock" is very popular in Paris, and the Ritz is one of the smartest if not the smartest place at which to drink tea. In the evening the big restaurant, with its ceiling painted to represent the sky and its mirrors latticed to represent windows, is always full, the contrast to a smart English restaurant being that three-quarters of the ladies dine in their hats. Sometimes very elaborate entertainments are given in the Ritz, and I can recall one occasion on a hot summer night, when the garden was tented over and turned into a gorge apparently somewhere near the North Pole, there being blocks and pillars of ice everywhere. The anteroom was a mass of palms, and the idea of the assemblage of the guests in the tropics and their sudden transference to the land of ice was excellently carried out. I give the menu of another great dinner at the Ritz because, not only has it some of the specialities of the house embodied in it, but that it is a good specimen of what a great dinner should be, being important but not heavy:—

Caviar frais. Hors-d'œuvre.
Royal Tortue Claire. Crème d'Artichauts.
Mousseline d'Eperlans aux Ecrevisses à l'Américaine.
Noisettes de Ris de Veau au fumet de Champignons.
Selle de Chevreuil Grand Veneur. Purée de Marrons.
Poularde de Houdan Vendôme.
Sorbets au Kirsch.
Ortolans aux Croûtons.
Cœurs de Laitues.
Asperges vertes en branches. Sauce Mousseline.
Ananas voilé à l'Orientale.
Friandises.
Corbeilles de Fruits.

VINS.

Château Caillou 1888.
Château Léoville Lascases 1878 (Magnums).
Lanson Brut 1892 (Magnums).
Château Yquem 1869.
Grande Fine Champagne 1790 (Ritz Réservé).

There are a score of capital restaurants in Paris which may be called "bourgeois" without in any way detracting from their excellence. An excellent type of such a restaurant is Maire's, at the corner of the Bd. St-Dennis, owned by the company which controls the Paillard's Restaurant of the Champs Elysées. It is a good place to dine at for any one going to the play at the Porte St-Martin, the Renaissance, the Théâtre Antoine, or any of the music halls or theatres in the west of Paris. Mushrooms always seem to me to play a great part in the cookery at Maire's, and the *Poulet Maire* is a fowl cooked with mushrooms; but the restaurant has a long list of specialities of all kinds, and the mushroom only appears in some of them. Charbonnier is the especial dinner wine of the house, and it is said that the name was originally given to the wine owing to the discovery of a quantity of it stored under sticks of charcoal in the days when Maire's was only a wine-shop.

Next door to the Gymnase Theatre is Marguery's, which always seems to be full, and where the service is rather too hurried and too slap-dash to suit the contemplative gourmet; but Marguery's has its special claim to fame as the place where the *Sole Marguery* was invented, and though I have eaten the dish in half a hundred restaurants, there is no place where it is so perfectly cooked as in the restaurant where it was first thought of, for nowhere else is the sauce quite as good or as strong.

Notta, 2 Bd. Poissonière, and Noel Peters in the Passage des Princes, both have claims to celebrity for their cooking, and the fish dishes at the latter, the *Filet de Sole Noël* for instance, are a speciality. The Bœuf à la Mode, Rue de Valois, near the Palais Royale, is a place of good cookery.

There are two restaurants to which I generally go if I want good food but have not time to linger over it, having cut my time rather close when going to a theatre or to catch a train. One of these is Lucas's in the little square opposite the Madeleine, and the other is the Champeaux, Place de la Bourse. Lucas has rather an old-fashioned *clientèle* and his restaurant is not very bright, but the cooking is good, and if in a hurry one is served very quickly. The *Hareng Lucas* is an exceptionally stimulating *hors-d'œuvre*, and there is a selection of old brandies to choose from as liqueurs which I fancy cannot be surpassed at any restaurant in Paris. The Champeaux, with its garden and trees growing through the roof, is the restaurant of the Bourse. It has a good cook, it has its specialities of cuisine, and it has a particularly good cellar of wines. One can dine there in the leisurely manner in which a dinner should be eaten by sane men; but the *maîtres-d'hôtel* used to business men know that there are occasions when it is necessary to be in a hurry, and they can serve a dinner very quickly. At the Champeaux, which has much history behind it, the *Chateaubriand* was invented which gives eternal honour to the restaurant.

I am told that Sylvain's remains a good dining place, but I have not been within its doors since the days when it attained celebrity as a supper place in favour with the butterfly ladies of Paris.

Across the River

On the south side of the Seine there are three restaurants worthy the consideration of the gourmet,—the Tour d'Argent, La Peyrouse, and Foyot's. The Tour d'Argent is on the Quai de la Tourelle, just beyond the island on which Notre Dame stands. It is a little old-fashioned place with a narrow entrance hall and a low-ceilinged parlour. Frederic is its proprietor, and since Joseph of the Marivaux died Frederic remains the one great "character" in the dining world of Paris. In appearance he is the double of Ibsen, the same sweeping whiskers, the same wave of hair brushed straight off from the forehead. He is an inventor of dishes, and it is well to ask for a list of his "creations," which are of fish, eggs, meat, and fruit, and are generally named after some patron of the establishment,— *Canapé Clarence Mackay, Filet de Sole Gibbs, Filet de Lièvre Arnold White, Œufs Claude Lowther, Poire Wannamaker,* and so on. A marquis, M. de Lauzières de Themines, has written a long poem about Frederic, which is printed on the back of the list of "creations," and an artist has painted a portrait of the great man which will be shown to you if you have proved yourself a real gourmet. Madame Frederic, or his daughter, will hold the canvas for your inspection, and Frederic himself, brushing back his whiskers, will stand beside it in order that you may see what an excellent likeness it is. It is as well to interest Frederic in the ordering of your meal, and if you give him an idea of your requirements, he will select two or three of his "creations" which will make up a perfect meal. I always ask for a *Filet de Sole Cardinal,* which is one of his best dishes, and look to him to group a couple of other *plats* with it to make a perfect breakfast, for I look on the Tour d'Argent as being a better place to breakfast at than to dine at, owing to its distance from the centre of Paris. Frederic thinking out his dishes drops into a reverie and turns his eyes up to the ceiling. I once took a lady to breakfast at the Tour—she had selected it as being quite close to the Morgue, which she wanted to see after lunch, having a liking for cheerful sights—and she had the daring to interrupt Frederic's reverie. "And for the eggs?" I had said insinuatingly to the creator of dishes, and he had dropped into deepest thought. "*Uffs à la plat,*" said the lady, who fancied we were both at a loss as to how eggs could be cooked. Frederic came back from the clouds and gave the lady one look. It was not a look of anger, or contempt, but simply an expression of pity for the whole of her sex. Frederic, as Joseph did, holds that a dinner to be good must be short, which is, I believe, the first axiom that every true gourmet should enunciate and hold by, and an excellent proof that he holds to his tenets was once given me. When the Behring Sea Conference sat in Paris, the

American and English members used frequently to dine together after their labours. Lord Hannen had heard of the Tour d'Argent, and sent his secretary, a clever barrister, to order dinner there for all the members. He went to the Quai de la Tourelle, saw Frederic, and sketched out to him a regular Eaton Square dinner, two entrées, a joint, sorbet, game, an iced pudding, a savoury, and fruit. Frederic heard him out, and then very politely suggested that he should go elsewhere, for such a barbarous feast could not be served in the Tour d'Argent. If you are in great favour Frederic will cook you a dish himself, and will bustle into the room with the "creation" in his hands and great beads of perspiration, drawn out by the kitchen fire, on his broad brow. I am sorry, however, to have to write that the last time I saw Frederic, at the close of 1902, he was very ill. He complained of his chest, said that the weather oppressed him, and lamented the death of Joseph which had taken a friend and a brother artist away. His hair had lost its bold curve and his whiskers their glory. I told him in all sincerity that he must get over his malady, for that as there are so few "creators" and great *maîtres-d'hôtel* left we cannot spare one of the most original and most accomplished of them.

La Peyrouse on the Quai des Grands Augustins, is a little house with many small rooms. It is known to the students of the "Quartier" as "Le Navigateur." It is a favourite resort of the members of the Paris bar, has its special dishes, one of which is, as a matter of course, *Filets de Sole La Peyrouse*, and a most excellent cellar of Burgundies and white Bordeaux. The Cérons at 3 francs is excellent money's worth.

The Restaurant Foyot is almost opposite the Luxembourg Gallery, and is a very handy restaurant to dine at when going to the Odéon. *Potage Foyot*, *Riz de Veau Foyot*, *Homard Foyot*, and *Biscuit Foyot* are some of the dishes of the house, and all to be recommended. The anarchists once tried to blow up Foyot's with a bomb; but the only person injured was an anarchist poet, who has so far been false to his tenets as to dine in the company of aristocrats, and was tranquilly eating a *Truite Meunière*, in company with a beautiful lady, when his friends outside let off their firework. The *hors-d'œuvre* at Foyot's are particularly good. It is, however, a restaurant at which it is exceptionally difficult to get one's bill when one is in a hurry.

Summer Restaurants

Of the restaurants in the Champs Elysées, Laurent's and Paillard's are the most aristocratic. At Laurent's I generally find in summer some of the younger members of the staffs of the Embassies breakfasting under the trees behind the hedge which shuts the restaurant off from the bustle of Paris outside. Of the special dishes of the house the *Canard Pompéienne* remains to me an especially grateful memory. It is a cold duck stuffed with most of the rich edible things of this world, *foie gras* predominating, and it is covered with designs in red and black on a white ground.

Paillard's *bonbonnière*, in the Champs Elysées, is in the hands of the company which also owns Maire's Restaurant, to which I have already alluded. M. Paillard and the company formed under his name settled a disagreement in the law courts, with the result that M. Paillard retained the restaurant at the corner of the Chaussée d'Antin as his property, and the company took possession of the Restaurant Maire and the Pavillion des Champs Elysées. This, however, is mere history, for the Pavillion serves its meals with all the quiet luxury of the parent house, and I have a memory of a *Potage Crème d'Antin* which was especially excellent.

Ledoyen's has attained a particular celebrity as the restaurant where every one lunches on the *vernissage* day of the Salon. At dinner-time, on a fine evening, every table on the stretch of gravel before the little villa is occupied, and the good bourgeois, the little clerk taking his wife and mother-in-law out to dinner, are just as much in evidence, and more so, than the "smarter" classes of Parisians. The service is rather haphazard on a crowded night, and scurrying waiters appeal to the carvers in pathetic tones to wheel the moving tables on which the joints are kept hot up to their particular tables. The food is good, but not always served as hot as it should be—the fault of all open-air dining places. The wine-list is a good one, and I have drunk at Ledoyen's excellent champagne of the good brands and the great years at a comparatively small price. Guillemin, who was cook to the Duc de Vincennes, brought Ledoyen's into great favour in the fifties of the last century.

The Bouillon Riche, just behind the Alcazar, with its girl waiters I have generally found even more haphazard than Ledoyen's. Its food is neither noticeably good nor is it indifferent.

The Ambassadeurs prides itself on being quite a first-class restaurant, and it is one of the special experiences of the foreigner in Paris to dine at one of the tables in the balcony looking towards the stage, and to listen to the concert while you drink your coffee and sip your *fine champagne*. I have kept the menu of one such dinner, very well cooked and well served in spite of the crowded balcony and general hubbub of the evening, on a Grand Prix night. What the amount of the bill was that the host of the party had to pay I did not inquire, but I feel sure that it was a very long one.

This is the menu:—

Melon.
Potage Ambassadeurs.
Hors-d'œuvre.
Truite Gelée Mâconnaise.
Ris de Veau Financière.
Demi-Vierge en Chaud-Froid.
Poulets de Grain Rôtis.
Salade de Romaine.
Asperges Froides.
Coupes Jacques.
Dessert.
Petites Fraises.

The cold trout was excellent, and the wine was De St-Marceaux '89.

The Alcazar has a restaurant somewhat similar to that of the Ambassadeurs.

Chevillard's, at the Rond Point des Champs Elysées, is not an out-of-doors restaurant, but it is a favourite place to breakfast at on the way out to the races. The cooking is good. Sometimes the restaurant is crowded, and it is as well to secure a table in advance.

There are half-a-dozen cafés, farms where milk is sold, and other refreshment places in the Bois; but the two restaurants which the travelling gourmet is likely to dine at are the Pavillion d'Armenonville and the Château de Madrid. The first is very "smart," and the glass shelter which runs round the little house is filled on a summer night with men, all in dress-clothes, and ladies in flowered or feathered hats. The world and the half-world dine at adjacent tables, and neither section of Paris objects. The tables are decorated with flowers, and two bands, which play alternately, make music so softly that it does not interfere with conversation. The cooking is good, and the prices are rather high. There are tables under the trees surrounding the building, and some people dine at these; but "all Paris" seems to prefer to be squeezed into the least possible space under the glass verandah.

At the Château de Madrid the tables are set under the trees in the courtyard of the building, and the effect of the dimly seen buildings, the dark foliage, and the lights is very striking. The Madrid has always been an expensive place to dine at, but its reputation for cookery is good. Last year I dined at the Château one hot summer's night and found there M. Aubanel, who had left his little hotel at Monte Carlo, during the great heats, to take temporary command at the Madrid, striving to serve a great crowd of diners with an insufficient staff of waiters. I trust that the proprietors have made better arrangements since to meet any sudden inrush of guests. The Madrid has a capital cellar of wine.

On a race-morning I have eaten a little breakfast, well enough served, at the restaurant of the Café de la Cascade.

Supping-Places

The fickle Parisian crowd changes its supping-places without any apparent cause. A few hundred francs spent in gilding a ceiling, a quarrel between two damsels in gigantic hats as to which of them ordered a particular table to be reserved, and the whole cloud of butterflies rises to settle elsewhere. Julien's, Sylvain's, La Rue's, the Café de La Paix, Maire's, Paillard's all had their time when there was not a vacant seat in their rooms at 1 A.M. Durand's, in the summer of '92, was the society supping-place. At the Café de Paris, where M. Mourier, a former *maître-d'hôtel* of Maire's reigns, the British matron and the travelling American gaze at the *haute cocotterie*—who patronise the right fork of the room as you enter. At Maxim's, any gentleman may conduct the band if he wishes to, and the tables are often cleared away and a little impromptu dance organised. At the Café Américain, the profession of the ladies who frequent it at supper-time is a little too obvious. You should take your wife to Durand's. She will insist on going to the Café de Paris. You should not take her to Maxim's, and you cannot take her to the Américain. Of course, the supping-places I have enumerated are but a few of the many, for there is no Early Closing Act in France, every restaurant in Paris keeps open till 2 A.M., and some later, and supper is to be had at all of them. Personally, I am never happier at supper-time than when I am sitting in the back room at the Taverne Pousset picking crayfish out of a wooden bowl where they swim in savoury liquid, pulling them to pieces, and eating them as they were eaten before forks and spoons put fingers out of fashion. The Restaurant des Fleurs, the newest of the Parisian restaurants, in the Rue St-Honoré, is making a bid with its decoration in the "new art" style to capture those who sup.

Miscellaneous

Since Cubat in dudgeon gave up his restaurant in the Avenue of the Champs Elysées, there has been no prominent foreign restaurant in Paris.

Cubat, whose restaurant in St. Petersburg is so well known, brought Russian cookery to Paris; but though the Parisians are fond enough of cheering for the Dual Alliance, they did not dip into their pockets to keep the Russian restaurant in existence. An expensive German restaurant, a relic of the last exhibition, showed its lights just off the great boulevards, but after a time disappeared. There are Viennese restaurants on the boulevards and in the Rue d'Hauteville, and Spanish and Italian establishments may be found by the curious who wish to impair their digestion. The Englishman or American who has been feeding on rich food for any length of time, often yearns for perfectly simple food. At Henry's, at the Club Restaurant, and at most of the English and American bars with which Paris is now studded, a chop is obtainable, and a whisky and soda which is not poison; but I, personally, when *Paté de Foie Gras* becomes a horror, truffles a burden, and rich sauces an abomination, go to one of the *Tavernes*, the Royale in the Rue Royale, or the Anglais in the Rue Boissy d'Anglas (where you get Lucas's food at lower prices than in the restaurant by the Madeleine), or into one of the many houses of plain cookery on the boulevards, and order the simplest and least greasy soup on the bill of fare, some plainly grilled cutlets, and some green vegetables. A pint of the second or third claret on the wine-card washes down this penitential repast. At Puloski's, an uninviting-looking little establishment in the Rue St-Honoré, I have eaten excellent dishes of oysters cooked according to American methods, and that dry hash which boarding-house keepers across the Atlantic are supposed to serve perpetually to their paying guests, but which an American abroad is always glad to meet. You will find a great variety of oysters, Marennes, Ostendes, Zélandes, at Prunier's, in the Rue Duphot, and the dishes of the house—soup, sole, steak—are all cooked with oysters as a foundation, sauce, or garnish. Prunier's is the house at which the travelling gourmet generally tastes his first snails, the great Burgundian ones with striped shells, or the little gray fellows from the champagne vineyards. If you eat Prunier's oysters you should drink his white Burgundy. If you eat his snails, you should drink his red wine, for he has some excellent red Burgundy.

Most travellers at least once in their lives go the round of Montmartre and its Bohemian shows. I have dined with the great Fursy in the restaurant attached to the Tréteau de Tabarin, and was given good substantial bourgeois cookery. I asked the singer of the "Chansons Rosses" how it was that he, who girds at all things bourgeois and commonplace, ran the restaurant on such simple and non-eccentric lines; and he shrugged his shoulders, which I took to mean that you may trifle with a man's intellect but not with his stomach. About two in the morning, in the upstairs room at the Tréteau, there is often some amusement forward. Upstairs at the Rat Mort, you may dine in comfort with *Soupe à l'Onion* and *Tournedos Rat Mort* in the menu; and at the Abbaye de Thélème, and at the Restaurant Blanche in the place of that name, you will find the artists and sculptors of the Butte.

In the Quartier, Thurion's in the Boulevard St-Germain is an interesting restaurant for a wandering Anglo-Saxon to become acquainted with, for there he will see most of the young Americans and English who are climbing up the ladder of pictorial fame. It is a Parisian "Cheshire Cheese." The floors are sawdusted, the waiters rush about in hot haste, and the chickens stray in from the courtyard at the back and pick up the crumbs round the tables. The place has its traditions, and you can hear tales of Dickens and Thackeray from the plump lady who makes up the bills.

Good Cheap Restaurants

I feel tempted in connection with this heading to write as did the naturalist of snakes in Iceland; but besides the *tavernes* and *bouillons*, which give wonderful value for the money spent but do not require any lengthy mention in a book dealing with temples of the higher art, there are one or two interesting *table-d'hôte* restaurants where the meals are very cheap.

One of these is Philippe's, on the first floor of the Palais Royal, next door to the Petit Vefour, and another is the Dîner Français, 27 Bd. des Italiens.

St-Germain

The Pavillion Henri IV., on the terrace of St-Germain, where every travelling Briton and American breakfasts once during his summer stay in Paris, is "run" by the management of the Champeaux, and one gets very excellent cookery and service in consequence, the prices not being at all exorbitant. One groans, sitting at the little tables on the terraces and looking at the view, to think of the chances some of our hotels near London, with even finer views, throw away through lack of enterprise.

St-Cloud

The Pavillion Bleu at St-Cloud, the proprietor of which, M. Moreaux, bought the greater portion of the "grands vins" of the Maison d'Or, deserves a special word of commendation.

N.N.-D.

CHAPTER II

FRENCH PROVINCIAL TOWNS

The northern ports—Norman and Breton towns—The west coast and Bordeaux—Marseilles and the Riviera—The Pyrenees—Provence—Aix-les-Bains and other "cure" places.

I propose to take you, my gastronomic reader, first on a little tour round the coast of France from north-east round to south-east, pausing at any port or any watering-place where there is any restaurant of any mark, and then to make a few incursions inland.

Calais is, of course, our starting-place, and here my experience of leaving the buffet at the Terminus and exploring in the town is that one goes farther and does not fare so well. The buffet at Calais always has had the reputation of being one of the best in Europe, and though the Englishman new landed after a rough passage generally selects clear soup and stewed chicken as his meal, it is quite possible to obtain an admirably cooked lunch or dinner in the room off the restaurant; and the cold viands, the cream cheese, the vegetables and fruit are all worthy of attention. The "wagons-restaurants" which are attached now to most of the express trains, no doubt have cut into the business of the buffet restaurant; but as a contrast to the ordinary British station refreshment-and dining-room the Calais buffet deserves to be mentioned.

Boulogne

At Boulogne there is a restaurant in the Casino, but I think it adds very little to the revenues of the establishment. Most people take their meals contentedly or discontentedly in their hotels, but the little restaurant on the pier, which used to belong to the widow Poirmeur but is now the Restaurant Garnier, with its miniature terrace and its windows which look out on to the waves when the tide is up, has an individuality of its own, and is one of the haunts of the gourmet who enjoys a meal with unusual surroundings. In the winter the little restaurant hibernates. If customers appear the wife of the proprietor cooks dinner or lunch for them, and cooks very fairly; but with the advent of summer a cook is engaged for the season, and it is a matter of importance to the sojourner in Boulogne whether that cook ranks as "fair" or "good." He generally is good. Fish, of course, is always fresh at Boulogne and generally excellent in quality, and the shell-fish are above suspicion—at least I never heard of anybody suffering from eating *moules*,—therefore a *Sole Normande* or any similar dish generally forms part of a *déjeuner* on the pier, and this with an *entrecôte* and an *omelette au rhum* makes a fine solid sea-side feast. The buffet at the station, since it was taken in hand by the South-Eastern Railway, is not the dreadful place of ill-cooked food it used to be. At the terminus of the tramway which runs into the forest a little *cabaret* gives a simple meal, and the trip out and back is the pleasantest short excursion from Boulogne. At Wimille it is wise to inquire what charge the new hotel proposes to make before sitting down to a meal. Ambleteuse is another little watering-place to the north on the coast. Here the mid-day meal at the principal inn is lengthy if nothing else.

Following the coast along, Paris-Plage has not as yet developed any restaurant of note, and the inn at Etaples, which is the town on the railway whence the walk or drive to Paris-Plage has to be undertaken, is more famous for having given shelter to generations of artists, some of whom have paid their bills with sketches, than for its food, though some of the best *pré-salé* mutton in France comes from the fields over-flowed by the estuary at high tide. A goodly proportion of the shrimps and prawns one has to pay so highly for as *hors-d'œuvre* in the restaurants of Paris come from Paris-Plage, Le Touquet, and their neighbour down the coast, Berk. Indeed, if any gourmet has a *penchant* for shrimps and asses' milk, Berk would be his paradise. Tréport requires no description, but

Dieppe

is a place of importance, and in the days of the Second Empire Lafosse's Restaurant in the Grande Rue used to be one of the very best dining places in the provinces of France. Good cooking is now to be looked for from Cabois, 74 Grande Rue, from Beaufils, Rue de la Barre, and from Lefebvre, Rue de l'Hôtel de Ville. M. Ducordet, the proprietor of the Grand Hotel, who was the happy man chosen to supply M. Félix Faure with a banquet when he visited Dieppe, caters for the Casino and the Golf Club. The Casino restaurant is worthy of all commendation. The buffet at the Gare Maritime is above the average of buffets in its cookery.

The restaurant of the Hôtel Château at Puys, a mile and a half from Dieppe, is owned by Mons. Pelettier of local celebrity, who has collected an excellent cellar of wine.

At Pourville, two miles from Dieppe, Mons. Gras is responsible for the entertainment at the Hôtel Casino. The restaurant has a special reputation, made by "Papa" Paul Graff, who was formerly one of the many *chefs de cuisine* of Napoleon III., and who left the Tuileries to keep the hotel. The proprietor is very proud of his kitchens and larders, and is delighted to show them to visitors.

Havre

is one of the towns in which the Englishman or American crossing to Southampton or coming thence often finds himself for some hours.

Tortoni's in the market-place has a reputation for good cooking, but judging from the two or three dinners I have eaten there, both *à la carte* and the *table-d'hôte* one at 5 francs, the cookery is of the good solid bourgeois order, eight courses and a pint of wine for one's money. In days long gone by there used to be this footnote to the *carte du jour* at Tortoni's, "Les hors-d'œuvres ne se remplacent pas," which was translated for the benefit of the English, "The out-of-works do not replace themselves." Tortoni's Hôtel Restaurant must not be confounded with the Brasserie Tortoni quite close to it, which is a bachelor's resort; but which I, as a bachelor, have found very amusing sometimes after dinner.

Frascati's Restaurant, an adjunct to the big hotel on the sea-shore, is the "swagger" restaurant of the place, and many a man who has come over by the midnight boat and has stayed for a bathe and a meal at Frascati's before going on to Paris by the mid-day train has breakfasted there in content. The *Ecrevisses Bordelaises*, the *Croûtes aux Champignons*, the *Salade Russe* here have left me pleasant memories. In the winter the *chef* retires to Paris or elsewhere, and the restaurant is not to be so thoroughly trusted; and sometimes when a crowd of passengers are going across to Southampton by the night boat to catch an American steamer, I have found the attendance very sketchy, owing to the waiters having more work than they can do satisfactorily. The restaurant is in the verandah facing the sea.

So much from my own experience. Other people with larger knowledge all have a good word to say for Frascati's, but all a word of caution as to its prices. It is wise to look at the price of the champagnes, for instance, before giving an order. The official dinners at Havre are always given at Frascati's, and it is here that the British colony holds its annual banquet on the King's birthday. I append a menu of a dinner of ceremony at Frascati's which, though it is miles too long, is a very noble feast:—

Tortue claire à la Française.
Crème Du Barry.
Rissoles Lucullus.

Caisses de laitances Dieppoise.
Barbues dorées à la Vatel.
Selle de Chevreuil Nemrod.
Poularde du Mans Cambacérès.
Terrines d'Huîtres à la Joinville.
Cailles de vigne braisées Parisienne.
Granités à l'Armagnac.
Faisans de Compiègne rôtis.
Truffes au Champagne.
Salade Chrysanthème.
Pains de pointes d'Asperges à la Crème.
Turbans d'Ananas.
Glace Frascati.
Dessert.

The Hôtel de Normandie is another hostel at which the cooking is good and the wines excellent. This is a menu of a *table-d'hôte dîner maigre* served there on Good Friday, and it is an excellent example of a meal without meat:—

Bisque d'Ecrevisses.
Reine Christine.
Filets de Soles Normandy.
Nouillettes Napolitaine en Caisse.
Saumon de la Loire Tartare.
Sorbets Suprême Fécamp.
Coquille de Homard à l'Américaine.
Sarcelles sur Canapé.
Salade panachée.
Asperges d'Argenteuil Mousseline.
Petits Pois au Sucre.
Glace Quo Vadis.

Petits Fours. Corbeille de Fruits.
Dessert.

The cooking at the Continental Hotel is reported as being good, but its wine-list does not meet with so much praise. The Burgundies, red and white, at the Hôtel du Bordeaux are highly praised.

One of my correspondents sends me an account of Perrier's, a little restaurant, which I give in his own words. "The quaintest and most original place in Havre is a little restaurant on the quay, opposite where the Trouville boats start from. It is known equally well as 'Périer's' or the Restaurant des Pilotes. It is kept by one Buholzer, who was at one time *chef* at Rubion's in Marseilles. He afterwards was *chef* on one of the big Transatlantique boats, where he learnt to mix a very fair cocktail. The entrance is through a tiny café with sanded tiled floor. Thence a corkscrew staircase leads to a fair-sized room on the first floor. All the food you get there is excellent, and *Bouillabaisse* or *Homard à l'Américaine* 'constructed' by the boss, is a joy, not for ever, but in the case of the first named, for some time. The house does not go in for a very varied selection of wines, but what there is is good. Ask for their special roll." The same correspondent goes on to tell me that the proprietor of the Broche à Rôtir at St-Adresse, who used to be his own *chef*, and attained much local celebrity, has sold the goodwill, but that the place is still to be commended, and that Béquet of the Restaurant Béquet can, if he likes, cook the best dinner in the department; but that you must find him in the mood.

Of cafés in Havre, the Café Prader, near the theatre, and the Paris are the two where the drinkables are sure to be of good quality.

ROUEN

At Rouen the gourmet has a right to expect the *Caneton Rouennaise* and the *Sole Normande* to be cooked to perfection; and outside the hotels, some of which have excellent cooking, there is a restaurant, the Français, in the Rue Jacques le Lieur, a street which runs behind the Hôtel d'Angleterre, parallel to the Quai de la Bourse. Of course the Rouen duck is not any particular breed of duck, though the good people of Rouen will probably stone you if you assert this. It is simply a roan duck. The rich sauce which forms part of the dish was, however, invented at Rouen. The delights of the *Sole Normande* I need not dilate on. A good bottle of Burgundy is the best accompaniment to the duck. The Restaurant de Paris, in the Rue de la Grosse Horloge, is a very cheap restaurant, where you get a great deal to eat at dinner for 2 francs, and where you will find the *Choux Farcies* and other homely dishes of Normandy as well as the excellent little cream cheeses of the country.

Crossing the Seine, one is in the land of cider and Pont l'Evêque cheese. At Honfleur you will find a very good *table-d'hôte* at the old-fashioned Cheval Blanc on the Quai; and at the Ferme St-Siméon up on the hill, in beautifully wooded ground, there is to be obtained some particularly good sparkling cider. Honfleur has a special reputation for its shrimps and prawns.

Trouville Deauville

During the Trouville fortnight, when all the world descends upon Trouville, the various big hotels and the Casino have more clients than they really can cater for. At the Roches Noires one is likely to be kept waiting for a table, and at the Casino a harassed waiter thrusts a red mullet before one, when one has ordered a sole. The *moules* of Trouville are supposed to be particularly good, and also the fish. There are *table-d'hôte* meals at the restaurants of the Helder and De la Plage, the second being the cheaper of the two, and food is to be obtained at the little Café Restaurant on the edge of the *promenade des planches*. But Trouville in the season may be taken to be exiled Paris in a fever, half as expensive again, and not half so "well done."

Of the little bathing-places immediately east of Trouville—Houlgate-Beuzeval, Dives, Cabourg—there is little or nothing to say. At Cabourg the Hôtel des Ducs de Normandie has some kiosks with a full view of the sea, where it is pleasant to breakfast, and the Casino can always be taken for granted as a *pis aller* at all these little bathing-places. The quaintness of the old inn Guillaume le Conquérant at Dives counts for something, and the 5 franc *table-d'hôte* dinner there is good of its kind.

Caen

Tripes à la mode de Caen may be a homely dish but it is not to be despised, and it can be eaten quite at its best in the town where it was invented. I have eaten it with great content at a bourgeois restaurant, opposite to the Church of St-Pierre, the Restaurant Pépin, if my memory serves me rightly, and a *Sole Bordeaux* to precede it. The proprietor, M. Chandivert, was very anxious that I should add a *Caneton Rouennaise* to the feast, but I told him that "to every town its dish." He gave me a capital pint of red wine, and impressed on me the fact that he had obtained a gold medal at some exhibition for his *andouillettes*. Caen is the town of the *charcutiers*, and you may see more good cold viands shown in windows, in a walk through its streets, than you will find anywhere else outside a cookery exhibition. Caen is an oasis in the midst of the bad cookery of Western Normandy; and the restaurant at the Hôtel d'Angleterre and the Restaurant de Madrid are very much above the average of the restaurant of a French country town. In both restaurants you can dine and breakfast in the shade in the open air, the Madrid having a good garden, the Angleterre a great tent in the courtyard,—a welcome change from the stuffy rooms, full of flies, of most Normandy hotels. I have a most pleasant memory of a *Homard Américaine*, cooked at the Hôtel d'Angleterre, which was the very best lobster I ever ate in my life. The old *chef* who made the fame of the Angleterre has retired, but his successor is said to show no falling off in the art of preparing a good dinner. I would suggest to the wayfarer to breakfast in the garden of the Madrid and dine at the Angleterre. There is a little restaurant, A la Tour des Gens d'Armes, on the left bank of the canal which is much frequented by students, and where an *al fresco* lunch is served at a very small price. The food is good for the money, and there is always a chance of finding some merry gathering there. A note of warning should be sounded as to the cider and *vin ordinaire* supplied as part of the *table-d'hôte* dinners in Caen, and indeed everywhere in Normandy. There is almost invariably good cider to be had and good wine on payment, but the cider and wine usually put on the table rival each other as throat-cutting beverages. Vieux Calvados is an excellent *pousse café*. It reads almost like a fairy-tale to be able to recount that the delicious oysters from the coast-villages of Ouistreham and Courseulles can be bought at 50 centimes the dozen or very little more.

Cherbourg

This calling-place for Atlantic steamers is a very likely place for the earnest gourmet to find himself stranded in for a day, and I regret that there is no gastronomic find to report there. A most competent authority writes thus to me on the capabilities of the place:—

"There are no restaurants, in the true sense of the word, in Cherbourg.

"The leading hotel, where most of the people go, and which is the largest, with the best cuisine and service, is the Hôtel du Casino. This hotel is managed by Monsieur Marius, and though partially shut during the winter season, travellers can always get a good plain dinner there. During the summer season, that is from May till October, the hotel is fully open, and has a *petits chevaux* room, entry free of course, and also good military music in the gardens, twice a week. The gardens are also very prettily illuminated very often, whilst from time to time firework displays help to pass away the evenings. The dining-hall faces the only nice portion of beach in the town, and being entirely covered in with glass, is warm in winter and cool in summer, when it can all be open. The meals are usually *table-d'hôte*, but it is possible also to order a dinner if one prefers to do so. Here also the traveller will find a little English spoken among the waiters and management, which may be useful to him. The wines are pretty good, but there is no very special brand for which the place is known; also good Scotch and Irish whisky can be obtained at a reasonable price; the hotel does not boast of any special *plat* either.

"The Hôtel de France, another fair-sized hotel, is the one patronised mostly by the naval and military authorities of the town, but is not so amusing a place for the traveller to stay at or dine at; though I understand that the dinner to be obtained there is in every way satisfactory.

"Finally, I might mention two other hotels at which one can dine comfortably; these are the Hôtel d'Amirauté and the Hôtel d'Angleterre, at both of which a good plain dinner is served.

"The chief joint obtainable here to be recommended is of course the mutton, as Cherbourg is noted for its *pré-salé* all over France; but beyond this the food is of the usual ordinary kind to be obtained in most French towns of this size."

M. Roche, who made a little fortune in London in Old Compton Street, has taken a little hotel near Granville, and as he learned cooking under Frederic of the Tour d'Argent, he may be depended upon for an excellent meal.

Breton Resorts

Of the land of butter and eggs I have not much to write. Correspondents at St-Malo say a good word of the feeding both at the Hôtel de l'Univers and the Hôtel du Centre et de la Paix; but I cannot speak of either of these from personal knowledge, nor do I know anything of Dinard, though it is said that the best cookery in the province is found there. Cancale of course has its oyster-beds, and the esculent bivalve can be eaten within sight of the mud-flat on which it erstwhile reposed. The one restaurant in this part of the world for which every one has a good word is that of Poulard Aîné at Mont St-Michel, where there is a cheap *table-d'hôte* and where a good meal *à la carte* is also to be obtained.

Artichokes, prawns, potatoes, *langouste*, eggs, lobsters, crabs, are good all along the Breton coast; and at Quimper, at the Hôtel de l'Epée, you can—if you are in luck—get fresh sardines.

Here is a typical Breton menu, one of the meals at the Hôtel des Bains de Mer, Roscoff:—

>Artichauts à l'Huile.
>Pommes de terre à l'Huile.
>Porc frais froid aux Cornichons.
>Langouste Mayonnaise.
>Canards aux Navets.
>Omelette fines Herbes.
>Filet aux Pommes.
>Fromage à la Crème.
>Fruits, biscuits, etc.
>Cidre à discrétion.

This is rather a terrible mass of food ranged in the strangest order, but I insert it to show the traveller in Brittany that he need never think his meal ended when he reaches the omelette, and that he had better take a gargantuan appetite with him.

Apart from being a good homely place to stay at, La Villa Julia at Pont Aven is worth a visit, for it has been the temporary home of many of the greatest French painters, notably poor Bastien Lepage. They are welcome, and are provided with studios, only being charged 5 francs a day "pension." "The country is charming" writes an enthusiastic correspondent "and one lingers there, and the food is excellent. Even were it not, dear old Mlle. Julia is worth a journey. She is one of the most delightful of French landladies. In the old inn the walls of one large room are covered with pictures and sketches given her by her *chers artistes*."

BREST

This great naval town has better cafés than it has dining or lunching places; the Café Brestois in the Rue de Siam, and the Grand Café in the same street being both good. Besides the restaurants attached to the Hôtels des Voyageurs, Rue de Siam, Continentale, and de France in the Rue de la Mairie, there are the Restaurant Aury and the Brasserie de la Marine, both on the Champ de Bataille, but I have no details concerning them.

Skipping Nantes as being out of the route of the Anglo-Saxon abroad, though in the Place Grasselin the Français and the Cambronne both deserve a word, and the Plages d'Océan which lie between Nantes and Bordeaux as being purely French, though Rochefort has a European reputation for its cheese, and Marennes for its oysters, I step down from the platform to make room for my co-author A.B., who will take up the parable as to

BORDEAUX

Bordeaux is, of course, the home of claret, and good feeding goes with good liquor, the combination being essential. The result is that here you can procure a good dinner with the best of wines, which being consumed, so to say, on the spot where they have matured, are in perfection both as to flavour and condition.

The Hôtel Restaurant du Chapon Fin, under the management of MM. Dubois and Mendionde, is perhaps the best in the town. Here an excellent dinner *à la carte* is to be had and the service is *très soignée*. The cellar comprises the finest wines of the Gironde, Lafite, Haut Brion, Latour, Margaux Leoville, etc., with Pommery, Mumm, Cliquot as champagnes.

But to my idea, any one asking for champagne at Bordeaux would order a pork pie at Strasbourg. The Chapon Fin is fairly expensive, but good food and good Lafite are not given away. The appointments of the hotel are excellent.

The Café de Bordeaux is a more popular establishment with brilliant decorations, and if you do not wish for an *à la carte* dinner, you are provided with a very good "set" *déjeuner* for 4 francs. Dinner can be had for 5 francs, with a concert thrown in.

Another good hotel and restaurant with fairly moderate terms is the Bayonne, also boasting of a fine cellar of wine and service *à la carte*. In fact many people aver that at the Bayonne one can get as good if not a better dinner than at any other restaurant in Bordeaux.

The Hôtel des Princes et de la Paix has the Restaurant Sansot attached to it, which is quite good.

The Restaurant de Paris, situated on the lovely Promenade des Allées de Tourny, is a first-class establishment with very moderate prices, where a capital *déjeuner* can be obtained for 2 francs 50 centimes, or a dinner for 3 francs. The proprietor, Mons. Debreuil, was *chef* at some of the best cafés in Paris, and he has a *clientèle* of many well-known epicures in Bordeaux.

All these restaurants have saloons for private parties in case you require them.

The principal *spécialité* of Bordeaux, besides claret, is lampreys, which, when cooked *à la Bordelaise*, are about as rich and luscious a dish as a most ardent candidate for a bilious attack can desire. If you are there in the autumn, don't forget to order *Cèpes à la Bordelaise*.

To the above of my worthy *confrère*, I would only add that the Chapon Fin is a winter garden, somewhat resembling the Champeaux Restaurant in Paris; there are rockeries and ferns, and a great tree-trunk runs up to the roof, the foliage and branches being no doubt outside. A speciality is the *Potage Chapon Fin*, a vegetable soup which is excellent. The restaurant of the Bayonne is in a great conservatory. Judging from the few meals

I have eaten at each, I should class the Chapon Fin and the Bayonne as being equal in cookery. The first floor of the Café de Bordeaux is now decorated with mirrors and white walls, after the manner of the *chic* Parisian restaurants, but the Englishman who wishes to drink whisky and soda there—an unholy taste in a wine country—and who demands a special brand and Schweppe's soda, should ask how much he is going to be charged for it before he commits himself.

Arcachon

Of cooking at Arcachon there is nothing in particular to be said. The place has a celebrity for its oyster-beds, and a great number of the oysters we eat in England have been transplanted from the bay at Arcachon to the beds in British waters.

Biarritz

The average of cookery in the hotels at Biarritz is very good, for the competition is very keen, and as money is spent by the handful in this town on the bay where the Atlantic rolls in its breakers, any hotel which did not provide two excellent *table-d'hôte* meals would very soon be out of the running. In the basement of the building in which is the big Casino, "Mons. Boulant's Casino," as the natives call it, is a restaurant where a *table-d'hôte* lunch and dinner are served; but *the* restaurant of Biarritz is the one which Ritz has established on the first floor of the little Casino, the Casino Municipal, where one breakfasts in a glazed-in verandah overlooking the Plage and the favourite bathing-spot, and at dinner one looks across to the illuminated terrace of the other Casino. The decoration of this restaurant is of the simplest but at the same time of the most effective kind, being of growing bamboos which form green canopies above the tables. Biarritz depends but little on the surrounding country for its food, as the Pays Basque gives few good things to the kitchen. Fish is the one excellent thing that Biarritz itself contributes to all the menus, and the *Friture du Pays* is always excellent. Here is a menu of a little dinner for three at the Ritz. The *Minestrone* is an excellent Italian soup (which, by the way, Oddenino of the Imperial in London makes better than I have tasted it anywhere else out of Italy); the veal, I fancy, came from Paris, the *ortolans* from the far south:—

> Melon.
> Minestron Milanaise.
> Friture du Pays.
> Carré de Veau braisé aux Cèpes.
> Ortolans à la broche.
> Salade de Romaine.
> Coupes d'Entigny.

I have not kept any bill for this, but I know that I regarded the total as moderate in a town where all things in September are at gambler's prices. The Royalty, in the main street at Biarritz, is the afternoon gathering place for the young bloods, who there drink cooling liquids through straws out of long tumblers, while the ladies hold their parliament at tea-time in Miremont the confectioner's.

Marseilles

Once more I step down from the platform to give place to my colleague A.B.

Two of the best hotels in Marseilles, with restaurants attached to them, are the Noailles and the Hôtel du Louvre; the latter is owned and supervised by Mons. Echénard, who with Mons. Ritz helped to create the popularity of the Savoy Restaurant in London, and is also his coadjutor in the management of the Carlton Restaurant; it is needless to remark that any cuisine that Mons. Echénard takes in hand is worthy of attention.

Mons. Echénard has lately acquired the Réserve at Marseilles—a very pretty café and garden about half-an-hour's drive from the Cannebière, along the Corniche Road; it stands in a commanding position, with a lovely view of the bay and the surrounding mountains. It has furnished apartments attached to it, and for any one having to stay at Marseilles, either while waiting for the *Messageries Maritimes* liner or for the arrival of a yacht, it is infinitely preferable to the hot, stuffy town, and would be an excellent winter quarter. Like many similar seaside cafés abroad, it has its own *parc au coquillages* or shell-fish tanks, and you here get the world-renowned *Bouillabaisse* in perfection.

The best shell-fish are the *praires* and the *clovisses*, about the same size as walnuts or little neck clams; the *clovisses* are the largest, and rather take the place of oysters when the latter are not in season, in the same way the clam does in America; others are mussels, oysters, and *langoustes*. *Langoustes* differ as much as a skinny fowl from a *Poularde de Mans*. Mons. Echénard gets his from Corsica, and you then learn how they can vary. He has also a *Poularde Réservé en Cocotte Raviolis*, which is a dish to be remembered; and a small fat sole caught between Hyères and Toulon is not to be despised.

I am free to confess that the *Tutti Frutti de la Mare*, or stew consisting of the many lovely and variegated small fish that are caught in those waters, has no charm for me. Personally, I would as soon eat a surprise packet of pins, but of course, *chacun à son goût*. Anyway, if you are stranded in Marseilles for an afternoon or longer, you could go to many a worse place than the Réserve.

I suppose it is not necessary for me to add to A.B.'s discourse any description of what *Bouillabaisse* is, or how the Southerners firmly believe that this dish cannot be properly made except of the fish that swim in the Mediterranean, the rascaz, a little fellow all head and eyes, being an essential in the savoury stew, along with the eel, the lobster, the dory, the mackerel, and the girelle. Thackeray has sung the ballad of the dish as he used to eat it, and his *récette*, because it is poetry, is accepted, though it is but the fresh-water edition of the stew. If you do not like oil, garlic, and saffron, which all come into its composition, give it a wide berth. The *Brandade*, which is a cod-fish stew and a regular fisherman's dish, is by no means to be despised.

Before leaving the subject of Marseilles and its cookery and restaurants, let me record the verdict of a true gourmet and Englishman who always lives the winter through in Marseilles. He writes me that in Marseilles itself there are no restaurants worthy of the name, the best being Isnard's (Hôtel des Phocéens), Rue Thubaneau, and another good one that of the Hôtel d'Orléans, Rue Vacon, where the proprietor and the cook are brothers and charming people.

Those adventurous souls who wish to eat the fry of sea-urchins and other highly savoury dishes, with strange shell-fish and other extraordinary denizens of the deep as their foundation, should go to Bregaillon's at the Vieux Port. It is necessary to have a liking for garlic and a nose that fears no smells for this adventure; but if you bring your courage to the sticking point, order a dozen *oursins*, a *petit poêlon*, which is a *tournedos* in a *casserole*, and a *grive*. Cassis is the white wine of the house; and it has some good Château Neuf de Pape.

CANNES

Cannes is the first important town of the Riviera that the gourmet flying south comes to, and at Cannes he will find a typical Riviera restaurant. The Réserve at Cannes consists of one glassed-in shelter and another smaller building on the rocks, which juts out into the sea from the elbow of the Promenade de la Croisette. The spray of the wavelets set up by the breeze splash up against the glass, and to one side are the Iles des Lerins, St-Marguerite, and St-Honorat, where the liqueur Lerina is made, shining on the deep blue sea, and to the other the purple Montagnes de l'Esterel stand up with a wonderful jagged edge against the sky. Amongst the rocks on which the building of the restaurant stand are tanks, and in these swim fish, large and small, the fine lazy *dorades* and the lively little sea-gudgeon. One of the amusements of the place is that the breakfasters fish out with a net the little fishes which are to form a *friture*, or point out the bigger victim which they will presently eat for their meal. The cooking is simple and good, and with fish that thirty minutes before were swimming in the green water, an omelette, a simple dish of meat, and a pint of Cerons, or other white wine, a man may breakfast in the highest content looking at some of the sunniest scenes in the world. There is always some little band of Italian musicians playing and singing at the Réserve, and though in London one would vote them a nuisance, at Cannes the music seems to fit in with the lazy pleasure of breakfasting almost upon the waves, and the throaty tenor who has been singing of Santa Lucia gets a lining of francs to his hat. Most of the crowned heads who make holiday at Cannes have taken their breakfast often enough in the little glass summer-house, but the prices are in no way alarming. The ladies gather at tea-time at the white building, where Mme. Rumplemayer sells cakes and tea and coffee; and the Gallia also has a *clientèle* of tea-drinkers, for whose benefit the band plays of an afternoon.

NICE

At Nice the London House is one of the classical restaurants of France, and one may talk of it in comparison with the great houses of the boulevards of the capital. I am bound to confess that the great salon with its painted panels, its buffet and its skylight screened by an awning, is not a lively room; but the attendance is quiet, soft-footed, and unhurried, and the cooking is distinctly good. It has of course its *spécialités du maison*, and classical dishes have been invented within its walls; but the man who wants to take his wife out to dine, and who is prepared to pay a couple of sovereigns for the meal, will find that he need not exceed that amount. Here is the menu of a little dinner for two which I ordered last winter at the restaurant. With a pint of white wine, a pint of champagne, a liqueur, and two cups of coffee, my bill was 46 francs.

Hors-d'œuvre.
Potage Lamballe.
Friture de Goujons.
Longe de veau aux Céleris.
Gelinotte à la Casserole.
Salade Romaine et Concombre.
Dessert.

The little Restaurant Français, on the Promenade des Anglais, is one of the cheeriest places possible to breakfast at on a sunny morning. In the garden are palm-trees, and the tables are further shaded by great pink and white umbrellas. A scarlet-coated band of Hungarians plays inoffensive music under the verandah of the house, and the page and the *chasseur* water the road before the garden constantly with a fire-hose, in order that the motor-cars which go rushing past shall not smother the breakfast-eaters with dust. Broiled eggs and asparagus points, a trout fresh from the river Loup—if such a fish is on the bill of fare—and some tiny bird either roasted or *en casserole*, with some light white wine, is a suitable meal to be eaten in this garden of a doll's-house restaurant. The house has its history. It was formerly the Villa Würtz Dundas, where so many art treasures were collected in the salons Louis XV. and XVI. Mons. Emile Favre, the new proprietor, has added considerably to the old house.

The Restaurant du Helder, the white building in the arcade of the big Place, has good cookery, and its *table-d'hôte* meals are excellent.

On regatta days the world of fashion occupies all the tables of the restaurant on the *jetée* at breakfast-time.

Two resorts patronised by the young sparks of Nice are the Régence and the Garden Bar. The subjoined menu shows what the Régence can do when a big dinner is given there:—

Hors-d'œuvre variés.
Consommé à la d'Orléans.
Bouchées Montglas.
Filets de soles Joinville.
Pièce de bœuf Renaissance.
Chaud-froid de foie gras.
Petits pois à la Française.
Faisans de Bohême à la broche.
Salade niçoise.
Mousse Régence.
Pâtisserie. Dessert.

The great confectioner's shop in the Place Massena and the Casino Municipal are always crowded with ladies at tea-time.

Beaulieu

At Beaulieu the Restaurant de la Réserve is famous. It is just a convenient distance for a drive from Monte Carlo, and the world and the half-world drive or motor out there from the town on the rock and sit at adjacent tables in the verandah without showing any objection one to the other. The restaurant is a little white building in a garden, with a long platform built out over the sea, so that breakfasting one looks right down upon a blue depth of water. There are tables inside the building, but the early-comers and those wise people who have telephoned for tables take those in the verandah if the day be sunny. There are tanks into which the water runs in and out with each little wave and in these are the Marennes oysters and other shell-fish. Oysters, a *Mostelle à l'Anglaise*—Mostelle being the especial fish of this part of the world—and some tiny bit of meat is the breakfast I generally order at the Beaulieu Réserve; but the cook is capable of high flights, and I have seen most elaborate meals well served. The proprietors are two Italians who also own the neighbouring hotel, and who take their cook with them to Aix-les-Bains when they migrate during the summer to the restaurant of one of the casinos there. A little band of Italian singers and musicians add to the noise of this very merry little breakfasting place.

At Villefranche there are two unpretentious inns where men with an unnatural craving for *Bouillabaisse* go and eat it, and return with a strong aroma of saffron and garlic accompanying them, saying that they have partaken of the real dish, such as the fishermen cook for themselves, and not the stew toned down to suit civilised palates.

Monte Carlo

The first time that I stayed for a week or so in the principality, I lodged at the Hôtel du Monte Carlo, on the hill below the Post Office. It was a dingy hotel then, not having been redecorated and brightened up as it has been now; but it had the supreme attraction to a lieutenant in a marching regiment of being cheap. When the first day at dinner I cast my eye down the wine-list, I found amongst the clarets wines of the great vintage years at extraordinarily low prices, and in surprise I asked the reason. The manager explained to me that the hotel was in the early days used as a casino, and that the wines formed part of the cellar of the proprietor—whether Mons. Blanc, or another, I do not remember. Most of them were too old to bear removal to Paris, and they were put down on the wine-list at ridiculously low prices in order to get rid of them, for, as the manager said, "In Monte Carlo the winners drink nothing but champagne, the losers water or whisky and soda." So it is. In Monte Carlo, when a man has won, he wants the very best of everything, and does not mind what he pays for it; when he has lost he has no appetite, and grudges the money he pays for a chop in the grill-room of the Café de Paris. The prices at the restaurants are nicely adapted to the purses of the winners; and there is no place in the world where it is more necessary to order with discrimination and to ask questions as to prices. At Monte

Carlo it is the custom to entirely disassociate your lodging from your feeding, and you may stay at one hotel and habitually feed at the restaurant of another without the proprietor of the first being at all unhappy. Ciro's in the arcade is a restaurant only, and is very smart and not at all cheap. A story is told that an Englishman, new to Monte Carlo and its ways, asked the liveried porter outside Ciro's whether it was a cheap restaurant. "Not exactly cheap," said the Machiavelian servitor, "but really very cheap for what you get here." On a fine day grand duchesses and the *haute cocotterie* beseech Ciro to reserve tables for them on the balcony looking out on the sea, and unless you are a person of great importance or notoriety, or of infinite push, you will find yourself relegated to a place inside the restaurant. At dinner there is not so much competition. Ciro himself is a little Italian, who speaks broken English and has a sense of humour which carries him over all difficulties. Every day brings some fresh story concerning the little man, and a typical one is his comforting assurance to some one who complained of an overcharge for butter. "Alla right" said Ciro complacently, "I take him off your bill and charge him to the Grand Duke. He not mind." The joke is sometimes against Ciro, as when, anxious to have all possible luxuries for a great British personage who was going to dine at the restaurant, and knowing that plover's eggs are much esteemed in England, he obtained some of the eggs, cooked them, and served them hot. Ciro's Restaurant originally was where his bar now is; but when the Café Riche, almost next door, was sold, he bought it, redecorated it, and transferred his restaurant to the new and more gorgeous premises, putting his brother Salvatore—who, poor fellow, has since died—in charge of the bar which he established in his old quarters. I cannot put my hand on the menu of any of the many breakfasts I have eaten at Ciro's, so I borrow a typical menu from V.B's. interesting little book *Ten Days at Monte Carlo*. He and three friends ate and drank this at *déjeuner:*—

Hors-d'œuvre variés.
Œufs pochés Grand Duc.

Mostelle à l'Anglaise.
Volaille en Casserole à la Fermière.
Pâtisserie.
Fromage.
Café.
1 Magnum Carbonnieux 1891.
Fine Champagne 1846.

This feast cost 61 francs. The Mostelle, as I have previously mentioned, is the special fish of this part of the coast. It is as delicate as a whiting, and is split open, fried, and served with bread crumbs and an over-sufficiency of melted butter.

At Monte Carlo one is given everything that can be imported and which is expensive. The salmon comes from Scotland or Sweden, and most of the other material for the feasts is sent down daily from Paris. The thrushes from Corsica, and some very good asparagus from Genoa or Rocbrune, are about the only provisions which come from the neighbourhood, except of course the fish, which is plentiful and excellent. I was last spring entrusted with the ordering of a dinner for six at the restaurant of the Hôtel de Paris, the most frequented of all the dining places at Monte Carlo, and I told Mons. Fleury, the manager, that I wanted as much local colour introduced into it as possible. He referred me to the *chef*, and between us we drew up this menu, which certainly has something of the sunny south about it:—

Hors-d'œuvre et Caviar frais.
Crème de Langoustines.
Friture de Nonnats.
Selle d'Agneau aux Primeurs.
Bécassines rôties.
Salade Niçoise.
Asperges de Gênes.

Sauce Mousseline.
Dessert.

Vins.

1 bottle Barsac.
3 bottles Pommery Vin Nature 1892.

To crown this feast we had some of the very old brandy, a treasure of the house, which added 60 francs to the bill. The total was 363 francs 10 centimes.

In this dinner the *Crème de Langoustines* was excellent, a most delightful *bisque*. The *nonnats* are the small fry of the bay, smaller far than whitebait, and are delicious to eat. They are perhaps more suitable for breakfast than for a dinner of ceremony, and had I not yearned for local colour I should have ordered the *Filets de Sole Egyptiennes* in little paper coffins which look like mummy cases, a dish which is one of the specialities of the house.

Dining at the Hôtel de Paris one pays in comfort for its popularity, for on a crowded night the tables in the big dining-room are put so close together that there is hardly room for the waiters to move between them, and the noise of the conversation rises to a roar through which the violins of the band outside the door can barely be heard. Bachelier, the *maître-d'hôtel* at the Français, a disciple of François, is quite one of the foremost men of his calling.

The restaurant of the Grand Hotel, where MM. Noel and Pattard themselves see to the comfort of their guests, is also a fashionable dining place. I first tasted the *Sole Waleska*, with its delicate flavouring of Parmesan, at the Grand Hotel many years ago, and it has always been one of the special dishes of the house. *Poularde à la Santos Dumont* is another speciality. This is a menu of a dinner for six given at the Grand, as a return for the one quoted above as a product of the Hôtel de Paris:—

> Crème Livonienne.
> Filets de Sole Waleska.
> Baron de Pauillac à la Broche.
> Purée de Champignons.
> Petits Pois Nouveaux.
> Merles de Corse.
> Salade.
> Asperges. Sauce Mousseline.
> Soufflé du Parmesan.
> Friandises.

The Hermitage, in which MM. Benoit and Fourault are interested, shares the rush of fashionable diners with Ciro and the Paris and Grand, but I cannot speak by personal knowledge of its dinners.

There are other restaurants not so expensive as the ones I have written of, and further up the hill, which can give one a most admirable dinner. The Helder is one of the restaurants where the men who have to live all their life at Monte Carlo often breakfast and dine, and Aubanel's Restaurant, the Princess', which one of the great stars of the Opera has very regularly patronised, deserves a special good word. The Restaurant Ré, which was originally a fish and oyster shop, but which is now a restaurant with fish as its speciality, is also an excellent place for men of moderate means. Madame Ré learned the art of the kitchen at the Reserve at Marseilles, and she knows as much about the cooking of fish as any woman in the world. When it came to my turn in the interchange of dinners for six to provide a feast, I went to Madame Ré and asked her to give me a fish dinner, and to keep it as distinctive as possible of the principality, and she at once saw what I wanted and entered into the spirit of it. She met me on the evening of the feast with a sorrowful expression on her handsome face, for she had sent a fisherman out very early in the morning into the bay to catch some of the little sea hedgehogs which were to form one course, but he had come back empty-handed. The menu stood as under, and we none of us missed the hedgehogs:—

Canapé de Nonnats.
Soupe de poisson Monégasque.
Supions en Buisson.
Dorade Bonne Femme.
Volaille Rôtie.
Langouste Parisienne.
Asperges Vinaigrette.
Dessert.

The *Soupe Monégasque* had a reminiscence in it of *Bouillabaisse*, but it was not too insistent; the *supions* were octopi, but delicate little gelatinous fellows, not leathery, as the Italian ones sometimes are; the *dorade* was a splendid fish, and though I fancy the *langouste* had come from northern waters and not from the bay, it was beautifully fresh and a monster of its kind.

The Riviera Palace has a restaurant to which many people come to breakfast, high above Monte Carlo and its heat, and the cook is a very good one.

Any mad Englishman who like myself takes long walks in the morning, will find the restaurant at the La Turbie terminus of the mountain railway a pleasant place at which to eat early breakfast; and the view from the terrace, where one munches one's *petit pain* and drinks one's coffee and milk, with an orange tree on either side of the table, is a superb one.

After the tables are closed the big room at the Café de Paris in Monte Carlo fills up with those who require supper or a "night cap" before going home; and though a sprinkling of ladies may be seen there, the half-world much preponderates. The night-birds finish the evening at the Festa, some distance up the hill, where two bands play, and there is some dancing, and where the lights are not put out until the small hours are growing into big ones.

Mentone

Mentone has a splendid tea-shop at Rumpelmayer's, and a pleasant restaurant at which to lunch is that of the Winter Palace. Many people drive from Monte Carlo to lunch or take tea at the Cap Martin Hôtel, and it is a pleasant place with a splendid view from the great terrace, though sometimes people not staying in the hotel complain of the slowness of the attendance there.

The Pyrenees

As a gastronomic guide to the Pyrenees I cannot do better than introduce to you my very good friend C.P., who knows that part of the world as well as any native, and whose taste is unimpeachable. I therefore stand down and let him speak for himself:—

Throughout the Pyrenees, in nine hotels out of ten, you can obtain a decently cooked luncheon or dinner—neither above nor below the average.

But in order to depart from the beaten track of the ordinary menu, abandon all hypocrisy, oh, intelligent traveller! and do not pretend that you can turn a fastidious nose away from the seductions of the burnt onion and the garlic clove, the foundations upon which rests the whole edifice of Pyrenean cooking. Pharisaical density would be only wasting time, for these two vegetables will be your constant companions so soon as you decide to sample the *cuisine bourgeoise* of the country. You should on no account fail to venture on this voyage of exploration, as some of the dishes are excellent, all of them interesting, and, once tasted, never to be forgotten.

To attempt to enumerate them all, to describe them minutely, or to give any account of their preparation, hardly comes within the scope of these notes. Suffice it to give the names of two or three.

First comes the *Garbure*, a kind of thick vegetable soup containing Heaven knows what ingredients, but all the same sure to please you. Next comes the *Confit d'Oie*, a sort of goose stew, utterly unlike anything you have tasted before, but not without its merits. Next, the *Cotelettes d'Izard mariné* may interest you. The izard, or chamois of the Pyrenees, has been *mariné* or soaked for some time in wine, vinegar, bay leaves, and other herbs. It thus acquires a distinctive and novel flavour. Don't forget the *Ragout* and the *Poulet*, either *chasseur* or else *paysanne*; nor yet the *Pie de Mars* if in season. By way of fish you will always find the trout delicious, either fried or else *à la meunière*. (Don't miss the *alose* if you are at Pau.) Lastly, the Pyrenean *pâtés, Gibier* and *Foie de Canard*, are justly celebrated, and can more than hold their own in friendly and patriotic rivalry with any of those purporting to come from Strasbourg or Nancy.

At first acquaintance you will not care much for *pic-à-pou* or the wine of the country, but with patience you may possibly learn to appreciate the Vin de Jurançon. Tradition has it that Henri Quatre's nurses preferred to give this form of nourishment rather than the Mellin's Food of the time. Perhaps babies were differently constituted in those days.

In any case you will always be able to get a good bottle of claret, bearing the name of some first-class Bordeaux firm, such as Johnson, Barton Guestier, or Luze, etc. If you are lucky enough to obtain a glass of genuine old Armagnac, you will probably rank it, as a liqueur, very nearly as high as any cognac you have ever tasted.

A word of warning! Don't be too eager to order whisky and soda. The "Scotch" is not of uniform quality.

So much for eatables and drinkables. A few hints now as to where you might care to lunch or dine.

Pau

To begin with Pau. There is really a great artist there—a man whose sole hobby is his kitchen, and who, if he chooses, can send you up a dinner second to none. His name is Guichard. Go and have a talk with him. Hear what he has to say on the *fond-de-cuisine* theory. Let him arrange your menu and await the result with confidence. That confidence will not be misplaced.

For purely local dishes of the *cuisine-bourgeoise* type, you might try a meal at the Hôtel de la Poste. But for general comfort the English Club stands easily first. The coffee-room is run admirably, and as for wine and cigars, they are as good as money can buy. A strong remark, eh? But true, nevertheless. For a supper after the play you might give a trial to the restaurant at the new Palais d'Hiver. Other restaurants are at the Hôtel de France and the Hôtel Gassion.

For confectionery, cakes, candied fruits, etc., Luc or Seghin will be found quite A1. Whilst for five o'clock tea, Madame Bouzoum has deservedly gained a reputation as great as that of Rumpelmayer on the Riviera. But again a word of warning! Be discreet as to repeating any local tittle-tattle you may possibly overhear. So much for Pau.

Throughout the mountain resorts of the Pyrenees, such as Luchon—Bagnères de Bigorre, Gavarnie, St-Sauveur; Cauterets—Eaux Bonnes, Eaux Chaudes, Oloron, etc., you can always, as was stated previously, rely upon getting an averagely well-served luncheon or dinner, and nothing more—trout and chicken, although excellent, being inevitable. But there is one splendid and notable exception, viz., the Hôtel de France at Argelès-Gazost, kept by Joseph Peyrafitte, known to his intimates as "Papa." In his way he is as great an artist as the aforementioned Guichard; the main difference between the methods of the two professors being that the latter's art is influenced by the traditions of the Parisian school, while the former is more of an impressionist, and does not hesitate to introduce local colour with broad effects,—merely a question of taste after all.

For this reason you should not fail to pay a visit to Argelès to make the acquaintance of Monsieur Peyrafitte. Ask him to give you a luncheon such as he supplies to the golf club of which Lord Kilmaine is president, and for dinner (being always mindful of the value of local colour) consult him, over a glass of Quinquina and vermouth, as to some of the dishes mentioned earlier in this article. You won't regret your visit.

In conclusion, should you find yourself anywhere near Lourdes at the time of the Pèlerinage National, go and dine at one of the principal hotels there—say the Hôtel de la Grotte. You will not dine either well or comfortably, the pandemonium being indescribable. But you will have gained an experience which you will not readily forget. *Adishat!*

Provence

Any one who is making a leisurely journey from Marseilles to the Roman cities of Provence, and who halts by the way at Martigues, the "Venice of Provence" should breakfast at the Hôtel Chabas; and if M. Paul Chabas is still in the land of the living, as I trust he is, and you can persuade him—telling him that he is the best cook in Provence, which he is—to make you some of the Provençal dishes, the *Bouillabaisse*, or that excellent *vol-au-vent* which they call a *Tourte* in the land of Tartaria, or the *Sou Fassu*, which is a cabbage stuffed with a most savoury mixture of vegetable and meat, you will be fortunate. At Arles the Hôtel Forum has a cook who is a credit to his native province; but if you stay in the house, make sure that you have a room to the front, otherwise you may only look into the well-like covered court of the house. At Tarascon, if you feel inclined to hunt for the imaginary home of the imaginary hero, a great man whom the town repudiates as having been invented in order that the world should be amused at its expense, take your meal at the Hôtel des Empereurs and ask for M. Andrieu. At Avignon the Hôtel de l'Europe is a very old-fashioned house with old furniture in the rooms, old latches to the doors. The servants seem to have caught the spirit of the place, and there is one old servitor, still, I trust, alive, who might have been the model for all the faithful old servants in the plays of the Comédie Française. The house is kept by an old lady; the cook is a man. Several people of my acquaintance choose Avignon as their halting-place on their way to the Riviera because of the quaintness of the old hotel and of the excellence of its cuisine. A breakfast on the Isle de Barthelasse, when the mistral is not blowing, is one of the holiday treats of the inhabitants of the town. At Remoulins the old Ledenon wine at the one hotel in the place is worth a note. At St-Remy, M. Teston, who keeps the hotel named after him, is an excellent cook. At Nîmes, at the Hôtel du Cheval Blanc, there used to be some excellent old Armagnac brandy, and probably some of it still remains.

"Cure" Places

Most of the French cure places are for invalids and invalids only, and the gourmet who goes to them has to lay aside his critical faculties and to be content with the simplest fare, well or indifferently cooked, according to his choice of an hotel.

Aix-les-Bains

The big Savoy town of baths is the principal exception to the rule, for the baccarat in the two Casinos draws all the big gamblers in Europe to the place, and one half of Aix-les-Bains goes to bed about the time that the other half is being carried in rough sedan chairs to be parboiled and massaged.

In the late spring there is an exodus from the Riviera to Aix-les-Bains; doctors, *maîtres d'hôtel* musicians, lawyers, fly-men, waiters move into summer quarters; and any one who has time to spare, and enjoys a three-day drive through beautiful scenery, might well do worse than make a bargain with a fly-man for the trip from the coast to the town on the banks of the lake. When a fly-man does not secure a "monsieur" as a passenger, he as often as not drives a brace of friendly waiters over just for company sake. Thus any gourmet who knows his Riviera finds himself surrounded by friendly faces at Aix-les-Bains. There are excellent restaurants in some of the larger hotels, and you can dine in a garden, under lanterns lit by electric light, or on a glassed-in terrace whence a glimpse of the lake of Le Bourget under the moon may be obtained; and there are at the big Casino, the Cercle as it is called, and at the smaller one, the Ville des Fleurs, quite excellent restaurants. These two restaurants are managed by first-class men from the Riviera—the proprietors of the London House at Nice and of the Reserve at Beaulieu, were, I believe, last year the men in command—and the King of Greece, who is a gourmet of the first water, sets a praiseworthy example when he is at Aix of dining one day at the Cercle and the next at the Villa. The prices are Riviera prices and the cooking Riviera cooking.

The Anglo-American bar, nearly opposite the principal entrance to the Cercle, a bar where a whisky and soda costs two francs, always has its tiny dining-room crowded. Durret's, also opposite the Cercle, a small restaurant, is good and cheap. There are half-a-dozen little restaurants in the street running down to the station, but the sampling of the most likely looking one did not encourage me to try any further experiments.

To keep up the illusion that Aix-les-Bains is a part of the Riviera, there is a Rumpelmayer cake-shop within two minutes' walk of the Villa des Fleurs.

Many of the excursions from Aix have a little restaurant as the point to be reached. At Grand Port, the fishing village on the borders of the lake of Le Bourget, there is a pleasant house to breakfast at, the Beaurivage, with a garden from which an excellent view of the lake and the little bathing place can be obtained. They make a *Bouillabaisse* of fresh-water fish at this restaurant which is well worth eating and which is generally the Friday fare there. At Chambotte, where there is a fine view of the lake, Lansard has a hotel and restaurant. At Marlioz, near the race-course and an inhalation and bathing establishment, the pretty ladies of Aix often call a halt to breakfast, *Ecrevisses Bordelaises* being a speciality. At one of the little mountain inns, I fancy that of La Chambotte, the proprietor has married a Scotch wife, and her excellent cakes, made after the manner of her fatherland, come as a surprise to the French tourists. The châlets at the summit of the Grand Revard belong, I believe, to Mme. Ritz, wife of the Emperor of Hotels, and the feeding there naturally is excellent.

Most people who go a trip to the Lac d'Annecy breakfast on the boat, though I believe there is a fair breakfast to be obtained at the Angleterre. On the boat a very ample meal is provided—the trout generally being excellent—which occupies the attention of the intelligent voyager during the whole of the time that he is supposed to be looking at waterfalls, castles, peaks, and picturesque villages.

VICHY

Outside the hotels, the restaurants attached to which give in most cases a good *table-d'hôte* dinner for six francs and a *déjeuner* for four, there are but few restaurants, for most people who come to Vichy live *en pension*, making a bargain with their hotel for their food for so much a day, a bargain which does not encourage them to go outside and take their meals. The Restauration, in the park close to the Casino, is a restaurant as well as a café, and is amusing in the evening. There are several small restaurants in the environs of Vichy. In the valleys of the Sichon and the Jolan, two streams which join near the village of Cusset and then flow into the Allier, are two little restaurants, each to be reached by a carriage road. Both the Restaurant les Malavaux near the ruins, and the Restaurant de l'Ardoisière near the Cascade of Gourre-Saillant, have their dishes, each of them making a speciality of trout and crayfish from the little river that flows hard by. At the Montagne Verte, whence a fine view of the valley of the Allier is obtainable, and at one or two other of the places to which walks and drives are taken, there are cafés and inns where decent food is obtainable.

Various

Men who know shake their heads when you ask them whether there is good food obtainable outside the hotels at Royat and La Bourboule, but I have a pleasant memory of an excellent dinner with good bourgeois cookery at Hugon's in the Rue Royale of the neighbouring town of Clermont-Ferrand. At Contrexeville I am told that the wise man finding his food good in his hotel, returns thanks and does not go prospecting elsewhere.

N.N.-D.

CHAPTER III

BELGIAN TOWNS

The food of the country—Antwerp—Spa—Bruges—Ostende.

I, the Editor, cannot do better in commencing this chapter than to introduce you to H.L., a *littérateur* and a "fin gourmet," living in Belgium, who has written the notes on "the food of the country" on Antwerp and Spa, and to whom I am indebted for the entire succeeding chapter on the Brussels' restaurants.

The Food of the Country

The Belgian is a big eater and a bird-eater. As a rule, in Belgium the restaurant that can put forth the longest menu will attract the most customers. There are people in Brussels who regularly travel out to Tirlemont, a little Flemish town nearly twenty miles away, to partake of a famous *table-d'hôte* dinner to which the guests sit down at one o'clock, and from which they seldom rise before five. The following is a specimen *carte* of one of these Gargantuan gorges served in December.

Huîtres de Burnham.
Potage Oxtail.
Saumon de Hollande à la Russe.
Bouchées à la Reine.

Chevreuil Diane Chasseresse.
Bécasses bardées sur Canapé.
Tête de veau en Tortue.
Surprises Grazilla (a Sorbet).
Pluviers dorés poire au vin.
Jambonneau au Madère.
Petites fèves de Marais à la Crème.
Salmis de Caneton Sauvage.
Faisan de Bohême.
Salade de Saison.
Dinde truffée Mayonnaise.
Glace Vanillée.
Fruits. Gâteaux. Dessert.

All this for five francs! with a bottle of Burgundy to wash it down, at any price from a crown to a pound. One thing that can safely be said about the Belgian restaurants is that a good bottle of Burgundy can nearly always be bought in both town and country. It is often told that the best Burgundy in the world is to be found in Belgian cellars. Whether this is a reputation maintained in honour of the Dukes of Burgundy who once ruled the land, or whether the good quality of the wine is due to the peculiar sandy soil, which permits of an unvarying temperature in the cellars, I will leave others to determine, but the fact remains that from a Beaujolais at 2 francs 50 centimes to a Richebourg at 20 francs, the Burgundy offered to the traveller in Belgium is generally unimpeachable. Ghent is another town famous for its big feasts. The market dinner on Friday at the Hôtel de la Poste is often quoted as a marvellous "spread," but the best restaurant in Ghent is undoubtedly Mottez's, on the Avenue Place d'Armes. This is an old-fashioned place with no appearance of a restaurant outside, and a stranger would easily pass it by. Here one dines both *à la carte* and at *table-d'hôte*; the *table-d'hôte* is well worth trying, though some of the dishes can be safely passed over. The wines at

Mottez's are very good, and some special old Flemish beer in bottles should be asked for. A great local dish is *Hochepot Gantois*, a mixture of pork, sausages, and vegetables which only the very hungry or the very daring should experiment upon at a strange place. Flemish cooking as a rule is fat and porky, and there is a dish often seen on the *carte* called *Choesels à la Bruxelloise*, which is considered a delicacy by the natives, and it is supposed to be a hash cooked in sherry or marsala; it is, however, a dish of mystery. A *plat* always to be found in Belgium (especially in the Flanders district), is *Waterzoei de Poulet*, a chicken broth served with the fowl. This is usually very safe, and any one going to Mottez's at Ghent should try it there. *Carbonades Flamandes* is another Flemish dish which, if well done, can be eaten without fear. This is beef-steak stewed in "faro," an acid Flemish beer, and served with a rich brown sauce. *Salade de Princesses Liégeoises* is a salad made with scarlet runners mixed with little pieces of fried bacon. The bacon takes the place of oil, while the vinegar should be used with rather a heavy hand. When other salads are scarce, this makes a really toothsome dish. Of all the Belgian *plats*, however, first and foremost must be placed *Grives à la Namuroise*, which of course are only to be obtained in the autumn. I have said that the Belgian is a bird-eater, and throughout the country every species of bird is pressed into service for the table. A stranger visiting the Ardennes will be struck by the remarkable silence of the woods, which is caused by the wholesale destruction of the birds. How the supply is kept up it is difficult to say, but no Belgian dinner is considered complete without a bird of some sort, and when *grives* are in season, thousands must be served daily. A *grive* proper is a thrush, but I fear that blackbirds and starlings often find their way to the *casserole* under the name of a *grive*. They should be cooked with the trail, in which mountain-ash berries are often found. These give the bird a peculiar and rather bitter flavour, but the berry that must be used in the cooking is that of the juniper plant, which grows very plentifully in Belgium. A traveller through Belgium in the summer or early autumn should always make a point of ordering *grives* at a good restaurant. When *grives* go out of season, we have woodcock and snipe; and there are several houses which make a speciality of *Bécasses à la fine Champagne*. At Mons and at Liège, and I think at Charleroi also, there is every year a woodcock feast, just as there is an oyster feast at Colchester. At these festivities a little wax candle is placed on the table beside each guest, so that he can take the head of his *bécasse* and frizzle it in the flame before he attacks its brains. Then we have plovers and larks in any quantity, but I would not like to vouch for what are often served as *alouettes* and *mauviettes*. The one bird that we never get in Belgium is grouse, unless it is brought over specially from England or Scotland. It has always been found impossible to rear grouse in the country. In the neighbourhood of Spa there are great stretches of moorlands reaching almost to the German frontier, covered with heather, which look as if they would be the ideal home of the grouse. Here M. Barry Herrfeldt, of the Château du Marteau at Spa, a real good sportsman, has tried his very utmost to rear grouse; first he laid down thousands of eggs and set them under partridges, but this proved a failure; then he introduced young birds, but they all died off, and I think he has now given up the attempt in despair. Whilst speaking of partridges, I ought to mention that there is no partridge in the world so plump and sweet as one shot in the neighbourhood of Louvain, where they feed on the beetroot cultivated for the sugar factories. At a restaurant *Coq de bruyère* is often served as grouse, but this is a blackcock. One last note: outside the capital and at all but the best restaurants the Flemish custom is to "dine" in the middle of the day and "sup" at about seven.

Antwerp

It is strange that a big city and seaport like Antwerp, which is a favourite stopping place of English and American visitors to the Continent, should have so few good restaurants. None of the establishments near the quays can be classed as even third-rate, and it is in the neighbourhood of the Bourse that the best eating-houses will be found. At the Rocher de Cancale, usually called Coulon's (after the proprietor), the cooking and the wines are everything that can be desired, but the prices can hardly be called moderate. This restaurant is situated at the corner of the Place de Meir and the Rue des Douze Mois, a little street leading down to the Bourse. On the Place de Meir itself is Bertrand's, another restaurant of the same high character, which, to the regret of its regular frequenters, is shortly to be converted into a larger and cheaper establishment. Everything at Bertrand's has always been first class, and local people who "knew the ropes" could get there an excellent *table-d'hôte* lunch for 3 francs. This *prix fixe*, however, was not advertised, and the stranger eating the same meal *à la carte*, would probably find his bill 10 or 12 francs without wine. Antwerp has a grill-room that can be highly recommended in the Criterium, situated on the Avenue de Keyser, near the Central Railway Station. The Criterium is also known as Keller's, and has a large English *clientèle*. Besides chops and steaks from the grill, there are other viands, and a *table-d'hôte* dinner is supplied in the middle of the day at 2 francs 50 centimes. The food is of the best, while a special feature is made of English beers and other drinks usually sought after by the Briton travelling abroad. The restaurant at the Zoological Gardens is well managed and much frequented.

Spa

"Les jeux sont faits! Rien ne va plus." It is not the cry of the croupier, it is the proclamation of Parliament. What will happen now that the Cercle des Etrangers at Spa has been closed, in consequence of the Belgian Anti-gambling Bill which came into operation on the 1st January 1903, it is difficult to say; one thing is certain, the hotels and restaurants will suffer, for more people came to the pretty little town on the outskirts of the Ardennes to try their luck at *roulette* or *trente et quarante* than to drink the iron waters at the Pouhon and other springs, or to take the effervescing baths and douches. Once upon a time, Spa was one of the most fashionable and most frequented watering-places in Europe, but gradually its glories have departed, although its natural beauties remain. Of the Spa restaurants as they exist today, there is little to be said and less to be praised. To tell the truth, there is not a really first-class restaurant in the place. To nearly all the springs, which are located in easy proximity to the town, so-called restaurants are attached, but the patronage being intermittent and uncertain, the choice of *plats* is limited, and the service is slow and bad. The Sauvenière Spring is nearest to the town, but the drive there is all up-hill, monotonous, and dusty. The Géronstère is more prettily situated, and is a favourite resort for luncheon during the summer season; but unless the meal is specially ordered beforehand, the visitor will, as a rule, have to be content with eggs, beef-steaks, or cutlets. The Tonnelet is situated on the roadside, and the restaurant there is often uncomfortable and dusty. Those who make the Tours des Fontaines will be best advised to stop for lunch at the Source de Barisart, which is situated in a most picturesque part of the woods, 160 feet above the town, from which it is distant about a mile. The much-written-of Promenade de Meyerbeer is close at hand, and a stroll beneath the trees before or after lunch will be enjoyed, for the surroundings are charming and romantic. If previous notice for a meal can be given, so much the better: there is probably a telephone from the town. In trout time this fish should be included, as it is caught plentifully in the district, and is, as a rule, fresh and good. As before said, there is no good restaurant in the town,— excepting, of course, those in connection with the principal hotels, where a *table-d'hôte* is usually served at mid-day and in the evening. The Café Restaurant attached to the Casino is convenient, and will be found more than sufficient now that the gaming rooms have been suppressed. On the other side of the Casino is the Hôtel d'Orange, well appointed and with a beautiful garden, and M. Goldschmidt, the proprietor, looks well after his guests. His dining-room has all the character of a restaurant, being open to the outside public. The company there is as a rule gay—sometimes, it is said, even a little too gay, but everything is of the best and well served. Probably, however, the gourmet will find things more to his taste at the

Grand Hôtel de l'Europe, where M. Henrard Richard always paid great attention to his cuisine. Although he no longer personally controls the management of L'Europe, the hotel is still under the direction of his family, and retains its high reputation. The following is a menu of a 6-franc *table-d'hôte* dinner served in September. It has not been specially selected, and is therefore a fair specimen:—

Bisque d'Ecrevisses.
Brunoise à la Royale.
Truites Meunière.
Filet de Bœuf garni Beaulieu.
Ris de veau Princesse.
Petits pois à la Française.
Perdreaux rôtis sur Canapés.
Glace Vanille.
Gaufrettes.
Corbeille de Fruits.

The wines here are good, the Moselle and Rhine wines being especially cheap. Other hotels with restaurants attached that may be mentioned are the Britannique (with a fine garden in which meals are served), the Bellevue, the Flandre, and the Rosette. The last mentioned is a small hotel attached to the Palace of the late Queen of the Belgians, and is run by Her Majesty's *chef*. The meals for the Palace were always cooked at the hotel, and the restaurant, though simply appointed, has latterly been excellent in its way. Strangers feeding there should try and secure a table on the little glass-covered terrace in front of the hotel. Mention might also be made of a couple of small restaurants that have in the past been supported by the professional players at the tables. One in a side street near the Casino, kept by a Frenchman, has a reputation for its cheap French wines; and the Macon, at a franc the bottle, is indeed drinkable. At the other, the Limbourg, the cooking is German in character and flavour. Both places may be recommended as wholesome and honest to people who want to "get through" on about 10 francs a day. There is no more to be said.

BRUGES

It always seems to me that Bruges is the quietest city in the world. At least when one sits out in the garden of the Hôtel de Flandre, after sampling some of the excellent old Burgundy which reposes in its cellars, and listens to the chimes from the brown belfry, a feeling of perfect peace steals over one. There are few hotels in Belgium, if any, which have such a fine selection of Burgundy as the Flandre has, and the food, if not noticeably good, is at all events not noticeably bad. Otto, who used to be the head waiter at the Hôtel de Flandre, is now the proprietor of the Hôtel de Londres in the station square; and though the appearance of the hotel is not inviting, he can cook a *sole au gratin* as well as any cook in Belgium. The *table-d'hôte* lunch at the Panier d'Or, in the chief square, is very excellent for the money.

OSTEND

I do not think that there is much to be said in favour of the restaurants of the big hotels at Ostend. One gets an imitation of a Parisian meal at half again the Paris price. I have little doubt that the cessation of gambling will bring all the prices down at the hotels, but during past years gamblers' prices have been asked and paid. At the Continental there is a 10-franc *table-d'hôte* dinner, much patronised, because people know exactly what it will cost them; and at the Palace Hotel there is a *table-d'hôte* room where the food served is well cooked; but it lacks the life and bustle of the restaurant, and most people who go there for a meal or two revert to the restaurant with its *à la carte* breakfasts and dinner. There is a Château Laroque in the cellars of the Palace at 7 francs a bottle which is quite excellent. There is a little restaurant, called the Taverne St-Jean, in a side street, the Rampe de Flandre, kept by an ex-head waiter from the Restaurant Ré at Monte Carlo, at which the cookery is thoroughly bourgeois, but good of its kind and the prices low; and there is on the quay a house, kept by a fisherman who is the owner of several smacks, where the explorer who does not mind surroundings redolent of the sea can get a good fried sole, and a more than fair bottle of white wine.

Any one who wishes to see what a Belgian meal can be in the number of courses should go by train past Blankenberghe, which is a pale reflection of Ostend, to Heyste, and partake of a mid-day dinner there at one of the hotels patronised by the Brussels tradesmen and their families, who come to the little sea-town for change of air. Fifteen or sixteen plates piled in front, or at the side of each place, mark the number of courses to be gone through, and most of the guests eat the meal through from soup to fruit without shirking a single course.

CHAPTER IV

BRUSSELS

The Savoy—The Epaule de Mouton—The Faille Déchirée—The Lion d'Or—The Regina—The Helder—The Filet de Sole—Wiltcher's—Justine's—The Etoile—The Belveder—The Café Riche—Duranton's—The Laiterie—Miscellaneous.

Brussels must have been a gayer city than the Brussels of today when it earned the title of "a little Paris." There is at the present time very little indeed of Paris about the Belgian capital, and, in the matter of restaurants, there is a marked contrast between the two cities. Here the latter-day Lucullus will have to seek in queer nooks and out-of-the-way corners to discover the best kitchens and the cellars where the wines are of the finest *crûs*. The aristocracy of Belgium mostly dines *en famille* and the restaurants that cater for the middle classes are the most patronised. There are, however, several establishments which provide for more refined tastes, but they will not be found upon the big boulevards or the main thoroughfares. Four of the best restaurants in Brussels are in two narrow little streets, and their exteriors resemble old-fashioned London coffee-houses, rather than resorts of fashion. Brussels is particularly destitute of smart rooms where one can sup in gay company "after the opera is over." Until the Savoy was opened, we had, in fact, nothing beyond the ordinary restaurant with its little *cabinets particuliers*. When Mr. Arthur Collins of Drury Lane was in Brussels about a couple of years ago, he asked me to take him one evening, after leaving the Scala, to the local Romano's. "We haven't such a place," I explained, "but we can go to the Helder." "I dined there this evening," said A.C., "it was a very good dinner, but deadly dull; show me something livelier." We resolved to try the Filet de Sole thinking, as it was close to the Palais d'Eté, we were certain to meet some people there, but the place was empty. The fact is, Brussels has little night-life beyond the taverns and bars of low character, and the only high-class supper-room is the Savoy. If a stranger came to pass a week in Brussels, and wanted to be shown round the restaurants, I should start him with lunch at the Savoy on Monday morning, and finish him off with supper at the Savoy on the following Sunday night, for he would then be sure of beginning and ending well. The grill is excellent, and by no means dear. 1 franc 75 centimes is charged for a chop or steak, including *pommes de terre* well served. The *hors-d'œuvre* are a speciality at luncheon. There is great variety, and the pickled shrimps would tickle the most jaded appetite.

On Monday night I should send my friend to dinner at the Epaule de Mouton.

On Tuesday, I should say, "Lunch at the Faille Déchirée and dine at the Lion d'Or."

On Wednesday, "Lunch at the Régina and dine at the Helder."

On Thursday, "Lunch at the Filet de Sole and dine at Wiltcher's."

On Friday, "Lunch at Justine's and dine at L'Etoile."

On Saturday, "Lunch at the Belveder and dine at the Café Riche."

On Sunday, "Lunch at Duranton's, and, if it is summer time, dine at the Laiterie."

He will then have sampled all the restaurants in Brussels that are worth troubling about, and will be very unlucky if he has not alighted upon some dish worth remembering.

The Savoy is situated in the Rue de l'Evêque, by the side of the General Post Office. It was originally a kind of offshoot from the American bar and grill-room of the Grand Hotel. Being done in good spirit and with good taste, it soon acquired favour, and at certain times in the day the premises are almost too small. There are private dining-rooms upstairs, and a restaurant on the first floor has lately been added. Everything is *à la carte*. The *café extra*, for which 75 centimes is charged, is a speciality. The manager is M.A. Reynier who speaks English like an Englishman.

The Epaule de Mouton is in the Rue des Harengs, one of the little streets already alluded to, which run from the Grand Place to the Rue Marché aux Herbes. In this street, which is barely five yards wide, are some of the best restaurants of the town; but the stranger must be particular and not enter the wrong door, as they are all huddled together, and the names of some of the establishments are very similar. There is, for instance, a Gigot de Mouton next door to the Epaule de Mouton, and there is a Filet de Bœuf. It is at the Epaule, however, where the best cuisine will be found. Behind the door on entering a snug corner for a *tête-à-tête* is to be found. Although the title of the establishment suggests Simpson's and a cut off the joint, the cuisine will be found thoroughly French, and everything is well and tastefully done. In ordering, it must be remembered that one *plat* is enough for two persons, and this is the rule in most Belgian restaurants. The Burgundy at L'Epaule de Mouton is renowned.

La Faille Déchirée is at a corner of another little street, the Rue Chair et Pain, close by the Rue des Harengs. The construction and decoration are quaint; one sits in a kind of tunnel and eats *Homard à l'Américaine* which is a speciality of the house. Woodcock, when in season, is also a dish to be ordered here.

Le Lion d'Or is a small establishment in the Rue Grétry, and may safely be called the "chic" restaurant of Brussels. The salon downstairs is a perfect little *bonbonnière*, and the rooms above are extremely cosy and comfy. The proprietor is Adolph Letellier (of course called simply "Adolph" by *habitués* of the house), and he is extremely popular among the young sports of the town. The *vrai* gourmet will appreciate *les plats les plus raffinés* on which Adolph prides himself. Everything is *à la carte*, prices being plainly marked. They are not cheap. The restaurant and rooms upstairs are open till two in the morning.

The Régina is a new restaurant at the top of the town, near the Porte de Namur. Although only opened in 1901, it has been found necessary to enlarge the premises, and the alterations are in progress at the moment of writing. When completed, the restaurant on the first floor will be more commodious and comfortable than it is at present. It is the good kitchen that has made the reputation of the place, and if this is maintained, the Régina will become one of the best patronised restaurants in Brussels. Some people prefer to feed in the café on the ground-floor but it is best to go upstairs, and, if possible, to obtain a table on the glass-covered balcony in the front, which has a pleasant outlook on the boulevards. The proprietor is Jules; he may have a surname but no one seems to know what it is; to one and all he is "Jules," a capital *patron* who, having been a waiter himself, knows how to look after the personal tastes of his customers. These include the officers of the grenadiers, the crack Belgian regiment, whose barracks are close by, judges and barristers from the Palais de Justice, members of the King's household (the royal palace being nearly opposite), actors from the Molière Theatre, sportsmen who foregather here on race-days, and the better-class Bohemians. Jules has also a good English *clientèle*, and makes a speciality of certain English dishes. This is the only place on the Continent I know which serves a really well-made Irish stew. The Flemish dishes are also safe to try here. The prices are very moderate, and the *plats du jour* range from 1 franc to 1 franc 75 centimes, each *plat* being enough for two persons. Breakfast dishes, such as *Œufs Gratinés aux Crevettes* and *Œufs Brouillés au foie de Volaille*, are also well done here. *Ecrevisses Régina* is a special dish of the house. There are always two special *plats du soir*. The Médoc de la Maison at 3 francs the bottle is a La Rose and is *very* good. Although the prices are low, there is nothing of the cheap and nasty order about the place. I have before me the bill of a little lunch for two served in December, which can be taken as a fair specimen of the fare and the charges:—

Huîtres de Zélande, 1 douzaine	3	frs.
1 bottle Sauterne	5	,,
Œufs en Cocotte	1	,,
Haricot de Mouton (plat du jour)	1	,,
Foie gras Hummel	2.50	,,
Salade de Laitue	1	,,
Laitance de Harengs	1.50	,,
1 bottle Médoc	3	,,
Café et liqueurs	2.50	,,
	20.50	frs.

At the same time, if one likes to lunch off a *plat du jour*, with a glass of Gruber's beer, it can easily be done at the Regina for less than 5 francs for two persons.

The Helder is in the Rue de l'Ecuyer, near the Opera House. It is a smart restaurant and one dines well there. It is frequented by a good class of people, but it has no particular character of its own. The proprietor is M. Dominique Courtade, formerly a *chef*, and he should be personally consulted if a special dinner is wanted. The Pontet Canet (only to be had in half bottles) should be sampled; it is very fine.

The Filet de Sole is in the neighbourhood of the markets and close by the Palais d'Eté. The proprietor is Emile Beaud. An excellent lunch can be obtained here at a fixed price, and one can also eat *à la carte*. Prices are lower than at most of the first-class restaurants, but the cuisine and wines are both safe and sound. The Cantenac at 4 francs is to be specially recommended, and the Médoc de la Maison at about 2 francs is also good. There are private rooms upstairs.

Wiltcher's, on the Boulevard de Waterloo, provides the best and cheapest *table-d'hôte* in Brussels. The price is only 3 francs, and is wonderful value for the money. The following is the menu of a dinner in January:—

Consommé à la Reine.
Filet de Sole à la Normande.
Quartier d'Agneau.
Mint Sauce à l'Anglaise.
Epinards à la Crème.
Poularde de Bruxelles en Cocotte.
Croquettes de Pommes de Terre.
Gangas du Japon à la Broche.
Compote de Mirabelles.
Salade de Laitue.
Glace Arlequin.
Biscuits de Reims.
Café.

In old Mr. Wiltcher's time a good many people came from outside for the excellent food here provided, but now so many families reside all the year round in the hotel, that it is difficult to get a table for dinner when it is not ordered beforehand. No matter what time of the year it is, there is always poultry and game on Wiltcher's *carte*, and one sometimes meets a strange bird here. Gangas is a Japanese partridge. The birds migrate to Northern Africa in winter and often cross to Spain, where they are caught in large numbers. The plumage of the gangas is very beautiful and the flesh is excellent eating. The outarde, or little bustard, is often to be had at Wiltcher's, and it is the only place at which I have eaten the great bustard, whose flesh is very much like a turkey's. White pheasant is another bird I remember here. Excepting in its plumage, it in no way differs from the ordinary pheasant. A feature of Wiltcher's dinner is that no fruit is ever included in the menu, although coffee is always served. The story goes that Wiltcher the First, who took great pride in his table, found it during one winter time almost impossible to give anything else as dessert beyond apples, oranges, pears, and nuts, there being no other fruit on the market. One day some diners rudely complained, and insisted on a change, expecting perhaps that pineapple should be included in a dinner at this price. "You wish a change in the dessert, I hear," said Mr. Wiltcher, in the suave and courtly manner which had earned for him the sobriquet of "the Duke"; "Very well, tomorrow you shall have a change." Tomorrow, there was no dessert upon the menu. When the reason for this was demanded, he simply answered, "You wanted a change, and you've got it. I shall give no fruit in future." This has become a tradition. Notwithstanding, it is a remarkable dinner, and there is usually a good variety of sweets. As a tip to people who want to drink champagne and are sometimes deterred by the high prices demanded for well-known brands, while being always suspicious of the sugary *tisanes* supplied on the Continent, I may mention that the champagne wines bearing Mr. Wiltcher's own name and labelled according to taste as Dry Royal and Grand Crémant respectively, are specially bottled for his establishment at Rheims; and, though the price is little more than half that charged for *les grandes marques*, they will be found pure, wholesome, and to the English and American taste. Wiltcher's is rapidly becoming essentially an American house.

Justine's is a little fish restaurant on the Quai au Bois à Brûler, by the side of the fish market. It has distinctly a bourgeois character. It is not the sort of place you would choose to take a lady in her summer frocks to, but you get a fine fish dinner there nevertheless. There is no restaurant in the world where *moules à la marinière* are served in such perfection, and you can rely on every bit of fish supplied there being fresh. The exterior is unattractive, even dirty, and the service inside is somewhat rough. On Fridays the place is always crowded, and there may be a difficulty about retaining a room upstairs, where it is best to go when you wish to be specially well served. In the old days, it was the fashion to go on Fridays (or on any day for a fish lunch) to Le Sabot, a *restaurant-estaminet* of the same order a little lower down on the quay, which has a reputation for its manner of cooking mussels; but, since the death of old François, who kept it, the place does not appear to be so much in favour, and the tide of custom now flows towards Justine's. It must be remembered that this house is mentioned simply as a feature of Brussels life and not as a representative restaurant.

L'Etoile, in the Rue des Harengs, is the most famous restaurant in Brussels. In the time of Louis Dot, it certainly held rank as the first of all, both for cooking and for wine, and Emile Ollivier, Dot's successor, is doing his best to sustain the reputation. Neatly framed and hung on one of the walls is still to be seen the card signed by the late Henry Pettitt, the dramatist, attesting to the fact that he had just eaten the best lunch of his life. This card some years later was countersigned by a Lord Mayor of London; and a Lord Mayor surely should be a good judge of a lunch. Whatever place is visited in Brussels, L'Etoile should not be missed. The stranger should be very careful to go in at the right door. The wines at L'Etoile have always been good, and Dot used to have some Burgundy that was world-renowned. His *fine champagne* was also famous, and he had some extra-special for which he used to charge 4 francs 50 centimes a glass. I have heard Dot himself tell the story how a well-known *restaurateur* from London came one evening with two friends to see how things were done at L'Etoile. After dinner they sent for Dot, to compliment him and ask him to join them with a liqueur, and he was to give them some of his best brandy. They smacked their lips on tasting it, and the glasses were filled a second time; but the gentleman who paid the bill rather raised his eyebrows when he saw the item, "liqueurs, 36 francs." "He got even with me, however," said Dot, "for when I went to London I returned his visit. I had a good dinner (not so good, I think, as I should have served), and I sent for him to join me with the coffee. While we chatted, I ordered cigars, repeating his words, 'Give us some of your very best.' He did, and he charged me 7s. 6d. a piece for them." The rooms at L'Etoile are very small, and if any one wants to prove the establishment at its best, he should take the precaution of retaining a table and ordering dinner beforehand.

Le Belveder is in the Rue Chair et Pain; it has lately been opened by Jules Letellier, *ex-maître-d'hôtel* of the Filet de Sole and brother to Adolph Letellier of the Lion d'Or. Here the restaurant is *à la carte*, and a speciality is made of fish and game. Things are well done, and it is a safe place to "take on."

The Café Riche is opposite the Helder, and nearer to the Opera House. It was founded in 1865 by Gautier, the nephew of Bignon of Paris, who retains the proprietorship and management until the present time. It has always had an aristocratic *clientèle*, and is specially favoured by Parisians visiting Brussels. During the political troubles in France the Duc d'Orléans, Prince Victor Napoléon, and Henri Rochefort were all patrons of the Café Riche, and it required all the tact and *savoir faire* of the proprietor to keep apart and at the same time give satisfaction and pleasure to the conflicting parties. The Café Riche is one of the best places in Brussels for a banquet or a large dinner-party. Woodcock and snipe *à la Riche* are specialities. Although the prices are generally *à la carte*, one can have a lunch and dinner at fixed price by ordering beforehand.

Duranton's, on the Avenue Louise, is now "run" by Monsieur Pierre Strobbe, who took a first prize at the Brussels cookery exhibition. The restaurant is pleasantly situated, and on Sunday, if you wish to go to the races in the afternoon, it is very convenient, being on the direct route to Boitsfort. There are three rooms on the ground floor, in which you can lunch. That on the right, a small narrow room under the orders of Charles, from the Black Forest, is the smartest. He will introduce you to some special Kirsch—from the Black Forest. The cooking in all the rooms is the same, and it is good. Order your cab to be at the door half an hour before the first race.

The Laiterie is in the Bois de la Cambre. In summer time it is indeed the most pleasant place to dine in Brussels. In the Bois there are several places that supply lunches, dinners, and light refreshments, but the Laiterie is the only one that is really first class. For seventeen years it has been under the management of M. Artus and his son. The establishment is the property of the town of Brussels, and is well kept up in every respect. Here on a Sunday as many as 1500 chairs and 400 tables are often occupied. In the evenings the gardens are brilliantly illuminated, there being 1100 gas lamps. Music is discoursed by a Tzigane orchestra, and the late Queen of the Belgians, who often used to stop her pony chaise at the Laiterie to hear them play, subscribed from her private purse 200 francs every year to these musicians. Dinners are served at separate tables, under Japanese umbrellas, and the cooking is excellent; but it is as well to secure a seat as near to the main building as possible, to overcome that objection to *al-fresco* meals—cold dishes. The wines are good, and M. Artus has some fine Ayala—'93, in magnums—unless it is all drunk by now. There must be something about the cellars of these out-door places peculiarly favourable to beer, for no pale ale in the world can compare with that drawn at the bars of the Epsom grand-stand, and in Belgium there is no bottled Bass so fresh and palatable as that which one gets at the Laiterie.

If my friend were staying in Brussels longer than a week, the other restaurants to which I might take him would be the Taverne Royale, at the corner of the Galeries Saint Hubert, where some real 1865 cognac can be had at 75 centimes the glass; the Frères Provençaux, in the Rue Royale; the Restaurant de la Monnaie (a large place, generally noisy, with not the most rapid of service); Stielen's, in the Rue de l'Evêque; and the Taverne Restaurant des Eleveurs on the Avenue de la Toison d'Or. At the Taverne de Londres, in the Rue de l'Ecuyer, there is always a fine cut of cold roast beef with English pickles.

On Wednesdays all the Brussels restaurants are crowded, it being Bourse day, and in a wide sense "market" day, when over 5000 strangers, mostly men, come into the city from provincial towns. In conclusion, I may mention that I have failed to discover the restaurant where George

Osborne gave his "great dinner" to the Bareacres a few days before the battle of Waterloo. Thackeray records that as they came away from the feast, Lord Bareacres asked to see the bill, and "pronounced it a d—bad dinner and d—dear!" Probably the place, therefore, is extinct; for happily the double pronouncement can nowadays be seldom applied to any of the restaurants mentioned in this chapter.

H.L.

CHAPTER V

HOLLAND

Restaurants at the Hague—Amsterdam—Scheveningen—Rotterdam—The food of the people.

THE HAGUE

At the Hague, the capital, the best restaurant is Van der Pyl's, in the centre of the town, situated on the Plaats, where the cuisine is French and excellent, and where there are admirable wines in the cellar. A good set luncheon is served at this restaurant for the very moderate price of one florin (1s. 8d.); but it is wise to order dinner *à la carte*, and to give them some hours' notice. The manager is M. Anjema. It is advisable to secure a table near the window, especially in summer. Some of the best wines are not put on the wine-list.

In former years the proprietor of Van der Pyl's was possessed of a puritanical conscience, and would not allow any two people to dine alone in his private salons. So strictly did he adhere to his rule on this subject, that when a well-known man-about-town insisted on his right to dine in the *petit salon* alone with his wife, the inexorable proprietor turned him out of the restaurant. There was, however, another well-known member of Hague society who succeeded where the gentleman who thought that matrimony overrode all rules had failed. The hero of the little story had made a bet that, in spite of the puritanical proprietor, he would dine *à deux* with a lady in the *petit salon*. He won his bet by subtlety. He ordered a dinner for three, and when he and the lady arrived they waited a quarter of an hour for the other imaginary guest. Then, remarking that he was sure Mr. X. would not mind the dinner being begun without him, the host ordered the soup to be brought up; and so, with constant allusions to the man that never came, the dinner was served, course by course, and the bet won before the proprietor had the least idea that a trick had been played upon him.

A somewhat similar story, it will be remembered, is told of Delmonico's and its proprietor in the early history of that great New York restaurant. In the American story, the youth who had dined in a *cabinet particulier* with a lady, in contravention of the rules of the house, had not the sense to hold his tongue until after he had paid his bill. When that document did make its appearance, some of the items were astonishing. "You don't expect me to pay this bill?" said the astonished diner to the proprietor, who had made his appearance. "No, I do not," said Mr. Delmonico, "but until you do you will not come into my restaurant again."

The following are some of the dishes Van der Pyl's makes a speciality of:—*Poule au pot Henri IV., Sole Normande, Côte de Bœuf à la Russe, Homards à l'Américaine, Poularde à la Parisienne, Perdreaux au choux, Omelette Sibérienne, Soufflé Palmyre, Poires Alaska*, most of them standard dishes of the usual *cuisine Française*, though the *Omelette Sibérienne* was invented to please a British diplomat who preferred a *soupçon* of absinthe to either rum or Kümmel with his omelette. And this is a typical menu drawn up by M. Anjema, a menu which reads as though it were for a French banquet:—

Huîtres de Zélande.
Caviar.
Consommé Diplomate.
Truite Saumonée à la Nantua.
Poularde à l'Impériale.
Noisettes de Chevreuil à la St-Hubert.

Délice de foie gras au Champagne.
Bécassines rôties. Salade St-Clair.
Tartelettes aux Haricots Verts.
Mousse Antoinette.
Sandwiches au Parmesan.
Dessert.

The Café Royal, in the Vijberberg, with an American luncheon bar on the ground floor and a restaurant upstairs, is fairly good.

Of the hotels to which restaurants are attached, the Hôtel des Indes and Hôtel Vieux Doelen have a reputation for good cookery. The former was in olden times the town house of the Barons van Brienen, and in winter many people of Dutch society, coming to the capital from the country for the season, take apartments there, and during that period of the year the restaurant is often filled by very brilliant gatherings. The manager, Mr. Haller, has been made a director of Claridge's Hotel in London, and divides his attention between the two hotels.

The following menu is a typical one of a dinner of ceremony at the Hôtel des Indes; it was composed for a banquet given by Count Henri Stürgkh:—

Huîtres.
Consommé Bagration.
Filets de Soles Joinville.
Carré de Mouton Nesselrode.
Parfait de foie gras de Strasbourg.
Fonds d'Artichauts à la Barigoule.
Grouse rôtis sur Croûtons.
Compote de Montreuil.
Cœurs de Laitues.
Crème au Chocolat et Vanille.
Paillettes au Fromage.

The Vieux Doelen has a beautiful old dining-room, and it is here that every year the smartest balls in the capital take place, given by the Société du Casino, and generally attended by Their Majesties and the Court.

Hock's fish shop in the market has a room where excellent oyster suppers are served, but this is not a place to which ladies should be taken at night, for it is then patronised by damsels who take the courtesy title of actresses, and the students from Leiden.

Amsterdam

The Restaurant Riche is managed by a Frenchman, and the cuisine is French. It is necessary to order dinner in advance, and it is well to be particular. Under these circumstances an excellent dinner is obtainable. There is a cellar of good wine, the Burgundies being especially to be recommended.

The Restaurant van Laar, in the Kalverstraat, has a celebrity for its fish dinners, and excellent oyster suppers are to be had there.

Scheveningen

Curiously enough, this important seaside resort has no restaurant with any claim to celebrity. The dinners to be obtained in the hotels have to suffice for the wants of the visitors to the place.

Rotterdam

The Stroomberg here deserves a word of commendation, the food to be obtained there being excellent.

The Food of the People

The cuisine of the country, the food the people of the country eat, is not recommended to the experimenting gourmet; for the favourite dish is a sort of Kedjeree, in which dried stock-fish, rice, potatoes, butter, and anchovies all play their part. Sauerkraut and sausages, soused herrings and milk puddings also have claims to be considered the national dishes.

CHAPTER VI

GERMAN TOWNS

The cookery of the country—Rathskeller and beer-cellars—Dresden—Münich—Nüremburg—Hanover—Leipsic—Frankfurt—Düsseldorf—The Rhine valley—"Cure" places—Kiel—Hamburg.

A German housewife who is a good cook can do marvels with a goose, having half-a-dozen stuffings for it, and she knows many other ways of treating a hare than roasting it or "jugging" it. She also is cunning in the making of the bitter-sweet salads and *purées* which are eaten with the more tasteless kinds of meat; but, unfortunately, the good German housewife does not as a rule control the hotel or restaurant that the travelling gourmet is likely to visit, but rules in her own comfortable home. The German Delikatessen, which form the "snacks" a Teuton eats at any time to encourage his thirst, are excellent; and the smoked sprats, and smoked and soused herrings, the various sausages and innumerable pickles, are the best edible products of the Fatherland. The German meat is as a rule poor. The best beef and mutton in the north has generally been imported from Holland. The German is a great eater of fresh-water fish,—pike, carp, perch, salmon, and trout all being found on his menus, the trout being cooked *au bleu*. Zander, a fish which is partly of the pike, partly of the trout species, is considered a great dainty. The vegetables are generally spoiled in the cooking, being converted into a *purée* which might well earn the adjective "eternal." Even the asparagus is spoilt by the native cook, being cut into inch cubes and set afloat in melted butter. *Compotes* sweet and sour, are served at strange times during the repast, and lastly, as a sort of "old guard," the much-beloved but deadly Sauerkraut, made from both red and white cabbage, is always brought up to complete the cook's victory. The potatoes in Germany are generally excellent, the sandy soil being suitable for their cultivation.

The cookery in the big hotels on much-frequented routes in Germany is now almost universally a rather heavy version of the French art, with perhaps a *compote* with the veal to give local colour. In the small hotels in little provincial towns the meals are served at the times that the middle-class German of the north usually eats them, and are an inferior copy of what he gets in his own home. As a warning I give what any enterprising traveller looking for the food of the country from the kitchen of a little inn may expect:—

Coffee at 8 A.M. with rolls, *Kaffee Brödchen*, and butter, and this meal he will be expected to descend to the dining-room to eat.

A slight lunch at 11 A.M., at which the German equivalent for a sandwich, a Brödchen cut and buttered, with a slice of uncooked ham, lachs, or cheese between the halves, makes its appearance, and a glass of beer or wine is drunk.

Dinner (Mittagessen) is announced between 1 and 2 o'clock, and is a long meal consisting of soup, which is the water in which the beef has been boiled; fish; a messy entrée, probably of Frankfurt sausage; the beef boiled to rags with a *compote* of plums or wortleberries and mashed apples; and, as the sweet, pancakes.

Coffee is served at 4 P.M. with *Kaffee Küchen*, its attendant cake, and at supper (Abendessen) one hot dish, generally veal, is given with a choice of cold viands or sausages in thin slices—*leber Würst, Göttinger Würst*, hot *Frankfurter Würst*, and black pudding.

If the above gruesome list does not warn the over-zealous inquirer, his indigestion be on his own head.

In the south the cookery, though still indifferent, approximates more nearly to the French bourgeois cookery.

A dinner-party at a private house of well-to-do German people is always a very long feast, lasting at least two hours, and the cookery, though good, is heavy and rich, and too many sauces accompany the meats. Many of the dishes are not served *à la Russe*, but are brought round in order that one may help one's self. Just as one is struggling into conversation in defective German, a pike's head obtrudes itself over the left shoulder, and it is necessary to twist in one's seat and go through a gymnastic performance to take a helping.

Except in large cities the Germans are not given to feeding at restaurants.

A golden rule, which may be held to apply all over Germany, is that it is safe to take ladies wherever officers go *in uniform*.

The Rathskeller

In most German towns where there is a Rathhaus (a town hall) one finds the Rathskeller, where beers or wine, according to the part of the country, are the principal attraction, single dishes, cutlets, steaks, cold meats, oysters, caviar being served more as an adjunct to the drink than as an orthodox meal. The most noted of these Rathskeller are at Bremen, Lübeck, and Hamburg, and that at Bremen is first in importance. It is a mediæval Gothic hall, built 1405-1410, and it holds the finest stock of Rhine and Moselle wine in the world. The wine is kept in very old casks. One of the cellars is of particular interest as being the "Rose" one, where the magistrates used to sit in secret conclave, *sub rosa*, beneath the great rose carved upon the ceiling. The German Emperor generally pays a visit to the Rathskeller when he visits Bremen.

In the Lübeck Rathskeller is the "admiral's table," said to be made from a plank of the ship of the last Admiral of Lübeck, who flourished in 1570;

and even more interesting than the Rathskeller is the Schiffergesellschaft, with its strange motto and its even stranger sign.

Beer-Cellars

Throughout Germany one meets in every town the large establishments, beautifully decorated in the "Old German" style, of the various beer companies, most of which are Munich ones, the Lowenbrau, the Pschorrbrau, the Münchener Hofbrau, and others. Be careful to close the metal top of your Schopps if you are drinking with German companions, for if you do not they have the right, by the custom of the country, to place their mugs on the top of the open one and demand another "round." If when you have emptied your mug, you leave it with the lid open, the waiter, without asking any questions, takes it away and refills it.

I now once more step down to allow A.B. to chat about the various German towns.

Dresden

Dresden is not exactly an epicure's paradise, but there is one restaurant which may, I think, be safely recommended as an establishment of the first order. I am referring to the Englischer Garten, which is managed by its proprietor, Herr Curt Roething. The principal entrance is through a rather dingy looking archway in the Waisenhausstrasse, nearly opposite the Victoria Salon Music Hall. The principal public rooms are on the ground floor. The decorations used to be of a very dismal type, but a year or two ago the rooms were all done up, and, without being palatial or particularly artistic, they are now quite nice and bright in their way.

There are also some rooms on the first floor which are generally used for private parties. The atmosphere in the winter is apt to be rather too sultry for English tastes, but it is perhaps less close than in most other

Dresden restaurants. At the back, there is an open space dignified by the name of a garden, running down to a nice wide street, and here in the summer a number of tables are laid, and one has the great advantage of dining *al fresco*.

The attendance is well above the Dresden average and the waiters there invariably clean and civil. The German waiter at his best is not often one of the highest polished specimens of humanity, although some compensation may be found in the almost paternal interest he takes in *habitués* or customers who have succeeded in winning his good graces. The table linen and other appointments are up to the mark without being luxurious.

In the middle of the day a huge dinner is served for 3s. By leaving out one or two courses, you can get quite as much as you can eat for lunch, and then you only have to pay 2s. This 2s. lunch is perhaps the cheapest, and, at the price, the best meal of its kind that one could possibly get at any restaurant. In its way, it is, I think, as remarkable a performance as the 1s. 6d. Sunday morning breakfast at the Grid at Oxford. It is, of course, not up to Chevillard or Paillard form, but quite good enough for ordinary requirements. In the evening everything is *à la carte*, and is almost as dear as the "set" meal in the middle of the day is cheap. Single portions are, however, with some very few exceptions, more than enough for two. The service is much more *récherché* than in the middle of the day; there is quite a large bill of fare, and you can get all ordinary restaurant dishes, in addition to a considerable selection of Delikatessen, such as oysters, caviar, fresh truffles, peaches, etc., all of which are kept in good qualities.

Game and fish are also good at the Englischer Garten, and the partridges and woodcocks are very well cooked; in fact, all their game can be highly recommended. Live trout and other fresh-water fish are kept in a tank, and you may generally rely on finding the soles and turbot fresh as well. As regards price, unless you are an *habitué* or make special terms, a fairly little simple dinner will average out at 10s. a head, exclusive of wine. It is well to order dinner beforehand, as the culinary arrangements are not very expeditious. In the evening the cuisine is by way of being first-class French art, but it just lacks the lightness of touch which is characteristic of the best French cookery.

Wine is rather dear, but the higher-priced brands of hock, Moselle, or claret are in some cases excellent. As to the champagnes found abroad, unless they are specially made for the English market, they must not be judged from an English standpoint, being as a rule far too sweet for our taste.

An instance of this occurred to me at Rheims, when staying with one of the champagne magnates for some shooting owned by a syndicate of some of the large champagne shippers. We met for *déjeuner* at their Châlet de Chasse or club-house, each gentleman bringing his own wine. The result was that one saw from ten to a dozen different famous brands of champagne on the table.

My host asked me which sort I would prefer. "Du vin Brut, if you have any," I replied. "Ah! Vous buvez de ce poison-là?" exclaimed he, smiling. So they evidently did not agree with our taste for dry wine. But you can make a pleasant and harmless drink of the sweet champagne in summer by mixing it with an equal quantity of light Moselle, adding a liqueur glass of curaçoa, and putting some wild strawberries or a large peach cut up into the concoction with some ice.

To return to the Englischer Garten. They also keep some particularly good Pilsen beer which they serve highly iced: that of course is as it should be, but it is apt to have disastrous consequences if one is not accustomed to it. Being a wine restaurant they do not expect you to drink beer except as a supplement to your wine, but if you make a point of it you can have it throughout. An additional charge of 6d. per head is made for the set mid-day meal if wine is not ordered.

The *clientèle* is by way of being "smart" in the evening, and there is generally a fair sprinkling of officers of the two crack Saxon cavalry regiments,—the Dresden Horse Guards and the Oschatz Lancers. Evening clothes, or, better still, a dress jacket and a black tie are advisable, but by no means *de rigueur*. The-cloth-cap knickerbocker-cum-Norfolk-jacket-get-up, unfortunately so frequently affected by travelling Englishmen in continental capitals, is certainly *not* to be recommended.

In the middle of the day the company is more bourgeois, and on Sundays, and occasionally on Saturdays, the place is apt to be unpleasantly crowded. In the evening, except on race nights, there is always plenty of room; in fact it is usually rather empty till after the plays are over.

The other restaurants would not appeal to a gourmet but, for a change, some of them are well worth visiting according to the season. For instance:—

The Belvedere, an old-established and very popular institution, delightfully situated on the Bruhlsche Terrasse, with a charming view over the Elbe and the principal architectural features of the town. Essentially a place for the summer, when one can take one's meals out of doors on its terraces and balconies. There is a beer and a wine department, and in the former an excellent band plays; but it is difficult to secure a table within earshot as there is always a great crowd. The attendance is indifferent and the cuisine fair and wholesome, though no doubt you could get a good dinner if you took a little trouble and ordered it.

The public dinners which take place there in the large banqueting hall are quite creditable productions, and the position, view, and fresh air all combine to render it a very pleasant hot-weather resort.

The Stadt Gotha. The wine restaurant is small and quaintly decorated. Very popular with the upper and middle classes and *extremely* respectable, cuisine very fair, set meals, and especially supper after the play very inexpensive. But if you order *à la carte*, like most other places, it is rather dear. A capital beer restaurant in connection with it and good; a thoroughly plain German cooking served here.

Tiedemann and Grahl's, in the Seestrasse, is a typical German Weinstube with a large *clientèle* of *habitués*, mostly men, but ladies can go there. The owners being large wine merchants have some first-rate wine at prices averaging rather lower than the Englischer Garten. But there is a very extensive list and the quality is not altogether uniform, so if you can suborn a friendly waiter he could help you considerably. Excellent oysters and smoked salmon are to be had here, but the place is apt to be rather crowded and noisy. The appointments are of the simplest and most unpretentious kind. Prices, moderately high—about two-thirds of the Englischer Garten. Set meals are served, but *à la carte* is more usual. The waiters, being institutions like most of the guests, are inclined to be a little off-hand and familiar, and there is altogether a free and easy and homely tone about the place, but it is perfectly respectable.

Neues Palais de Saxe, on the Neumarket, is owned and managed by Herr Muller. Very fair cuisine; good set meals; *à la carte* rather more expensive; speciality made of oysters and *écrevisses*, which latter are served in all sorts of fascinating ways. Not at all a bad place for supper after the theatre, but perhaps a trifle dull.

Kneist, in a little street off the Altmarkt, called, I think, the Grosse Brudergasse, is managed by the proprietor whose name it bears. This may perhaps be called the leading beer restaurant of Dresden; it is remarkably popular and considered very good. Worth a visit as a typical though favourable specimen of its kind. Much frequented by officers and officials; here you find good plain fare served in the simplest of fashions. Meals *à la carte* and quite inexpensive; cuisine purely German, homely and wholesome, with excellent beer, especially Erlanger. The atmosphere is usually hot, thick, and stuffy, but the *clientèle* does not seem to mind it.

In a little back room the principal dignitaries of the Saxon Court, State, and Army are wont to forgather every morning for their Frühschoppen,— a kind of early, largely liquid lunch, where, if rumour can be trusted, a good deal of important business is informally discussed and settled.

The Kaiser Palast, on the Pirnaischerplatz, is a huge but not particularly attractive establishment with wine and beer departments.

The best Pilsen beer in Dresden is obtainable at the Bierstall in a little street off the Altmarkt, in a somewhat disreputable quarter of the town;

it is not a suitable place for ladies, but is quite respectable for men. The beer is well worth sampling, but the air is not fit to breathe.

Good Munich beer is to be had at the Zacherlbrau in the König Johann Strasse.

As regards dining at hotels.

The Savoy (Sedanstrasse), the Europaischen Hof (Pragerstrasse), and the Bellevue (Theaterplatz) rank about equal. The set meals are of the usual hotel type; the *à la carte* prices are, of course, high. The preference of the English is generally given to the Savoy, but the Europaischer Hof is the most popular with German society. The Bellevue is very pleasant in the summer, having a large verandah with a lovely view overlooking the Elbe, where one can dine in the hot weather.

Munich

There are no absolutely first-class restaurants in Munich, although the Hôtel de Russie is certainly the best and now boasts of a capital *chef*. It is under the same directorate as the Vierjahrzeiten, but being a better class of establishment, with more modern appointments, it has eclipsed the latter. It is now a case of the Vierjahrzeiten's nose being put out of joint by its own child. Yet the latter, though rather old-fashioned, is still very comfortable and has an American bar.

Schleich's Restaurant is very good, as is also the Continental, on the Maximiliens Platz, and the Hungärische Hof.

You should visit the Hofbrauhaus in the Platz, if only to drink as good a glass of beer as one could wish to have. It is a fine and typical specimen of a German Bierhalle, very respectable and much frequented. After having had your first Schoppen (for having once tasted you invariably want more) you rinse out your glass at a handy fountain before presenting it to be refilled; but the person who takes your Schoppen along with several others in each hand, invariably with unerring instinct hands you back your same Schoppen. As an appetizer for the beer to which it is supposed to give an additional zest, they place a large radish about the size of an apple in a sort of turnip-cutting machine which ejects it in thin rings; it is then washed and put into a saucer with a little salt and water and eaten without any other accompaniment than the beer; it may be an acquired taste, but it appears to be very popular.

Nüremberg

Nüremberg being essentially a commercial and industrial town, it follows that expensive restaurants and high living are not one of the features of it. Yet the Bierkellers there are institutions that have existed since the time of Albert Dürer and his companions.

Among the best of these is the Rathhauskeller (or town-hall cellar), kept by Carl Giessing, a most picturesque place, as indeed is everything in Nüremberg; also the Fottinger in the Königstrasse and the Herrenkeller in the Theaterstrasse. At all of these good meals can be obtained at moderate prices, and hock is the best wine to order.

Perhaps the most interesting place in this storehouse of beautiful antiquities is the hostelry known as the Bratwurstglöcklein, or Little Bell of the Roast Sausage; here the specialities are excellent beer and the very best of diminutive sausages made fresh every day, also Sauerkraut. The bell is still suspended on the end wall by an ornamental, hammered iron bracket. Built about the year 1400, it is one of the most ancient, if not the oldest, refreshment house in the world, and has been used as such ever since. Here did the Meistersingers forgather, Hans Sachs, Peter Vischer, Albrecht Dürer, Wellebald Pirkheimer, Veit Stoss and other celebrated men in Nüremberg's history in the fifteenth and sixteenth centuries. Great historical interest has always attached to this house, where the best class of entertainment is to be had. The present owners profess to have many of the original drinking-mugs, cans, etc., that these old customers habitually used and which were individually reserved for them. The proprietors of the Bratwurstglöcklein are so particular with regard to the character of their sausages that they are made twice a day. Consequently the sausage they give you in the evening has not even been made that morning; it dates its construction only from mid-day.

There is a doggerel rhyme written of the establishment that runs very much in the same strain in which I have translated it:—

Not many noble strangers
Can possibly refrain,
When once they've ate our sausages
From eating them again.
And it usually strikes them,
If they have not yet found it out,
That these sausages are splendid
When they're mixed with Sauerkraut.
The only thing they rail at,
When they fain would criticise,
Is to wish the little sausage
Were a little larger size.

At the principal hotels, such as the Grand, Strauss, Württemberger Hof, and Victoria, very good meals can be procured—the mid-day *table-d'hôte* prices varying from 3s. to 3s. 6d. Perhaps the best of these is the Victoria, which rejoices in a grill-room, and where the delicacies of the season are available.

There are American bars at the "American Bar," Karolinenstrasse, the Hôtel Strauss, same street, and at the Wittelsbacker Hof in the Pfaunenschmiedsgasse.

The cafés are the Bristol in the Josephs Platz, the Central in the Karolinenstrasse, the Habsburg and the Imperial both in the Königstrasse; but do not go to any of these under the idea that they represent the Café Anglais in Paris.

A very pleasant resort in the summer is the Maxfeld Restauration in the Stadt Park. It is in the open air, and an excellent band plays at 5 P.M. on Tuesdays, Thursdays, and Sundays. A fair dinner is provided, but it is better to order in advance by telephone.

Hanover

The Georgshalle is, and has been for the last forty years, the best café and restaurant in Hanover, but is now incorporated with Kasten's Hotel. It was the usual and, for many years, the only place of resort where a simple and decent meal could be obtained. I am not talking of the *haute cuisine*, because it does not exist in this city.

Kasten's Hotel is good of its kind. The Kaiser has dined there on his occasional visits to the town. Private balls and other entertainments are given there, and the wines are generally good.

The Tip Top Restaurant, in the Karmarschstrasse, is a comparatively modern, pleasant, and cheery *locale*, with a good bill of fare. On account of its proximity to the theatre it is much frequented for suppers after the play.

There are several Biergärten open in the summer where military and other bands perform, but nothing but ordinary refreshment is to be obtained here.

Leipzig

Leipzig has one good restaurant, the Restaurant Päge on the Marktplatz,—at least it is the best in the town.

The Hôtel Hauffe, in the Russplatz, is an old-established hotel, is well conducted, and has a restaurant where one can get quite a decent dinner if ordered beforehand.

There is also another, Friedrichkrause, Katharinensbresse, No. 6, but with these three the culinary capabilities of Leipzig are practically at an end. Of course there are a number of Bierhalle and Kellern to accommodate the students and music pupils, for which latter Leipzig is the home of instruction.

Frankfurt-am-Main

Frankfurt gives me the idea of having more wealthy people in it than any other town I know, and I do not think I am very far wrong in this. The Central Railway Station is the finest one can imagine.

It has at least four first-class restaurants attached to hotels.

The Hôtel d'Angleterre, or Englischer Hof, in the centre of the city, the Rossmarkt, is a fine old hotel. Our present king, when Prince of Wales, generally stayed there when passing through. The famous German philosopher, Schopenhauer, dined there regularly for thirty years—from 1831 to 1860, though I cannot advance that as any great recommendation, for the ways and tastes of philosophers are usually somewhat erratic. I have no doubt, however, that the cuisine has materially altered since Schopenhauer's time.

The Frankfurter Hof, built about thirty years ago, is a larger establishment with all the modern improvements. It is much frequented by Englishmen and Americans, but rather lacks the quiet of the Angleterre. It has a good cuisine, for M. Ritz, who has an interest in the hotel, has seen to that, and magnificent reception rooms where many balls, parties, weddings, etc., take place. A band plays there during the greater part of the day, and it is advisable to get as far distant as possible from it when dining. In the restaurant one can obtain *à la carte* a very excellently cooked dinner.

The Palast Hôtel Furstenhof is of the highest class and was only recently opened. It has beautifully decorated rooms, a good restaurant, a dining-hall, and an excellent American bar. Herr Schill the former head waiter of the Englischer Hof—his *nom de guerre* is Mons. Jules—

assiduously sees to the comfort and welfare of his guests. Like Mons. Ritz he has a large following of friends.

The Hôtel Imperial was opened about two years ago, and although a little smaller than the Frankfurter Hof or the Palast has a most aristocratic *clientèle*. Being close to the Opera House, its restaurant is much patronised in the season by people who during the *entr'acte*, or to pass over a more or less tedious act, prefer to partake of light refreshments and a cigarette on the terrace in the open air. There is an American bar there also. The *élite* of Frankfurt, on the rare occasions when they do sup after going to the theatre or opera, generally order their meals at one of the restaurants of the leading hotels; but Frankfurt does not, as a rule, keep late hours.

The Palmen Garten is a pleasant summer restaurant a little way out of the town, on the Bockenheimerstrasse. It has a fine dining-hall, or you may sit at *al-fresco* tables while the regimental band discourses excellent music. The cooking is good—German cuisine, but nothing high class. It is a very pleasant spot to visit in the hot weather; on fête days one is treated there to the luxury of fireworks, etc.

Buerose ought to be mentioned as a quiet restaurant, where there is a *spécialité* of *hors-d'œuvre* and excellent oysters.

Lovers of good beer will find at the Allemania, if they ask for a Schoppen of the Royal Court Hofbrau, exactly what they have been craving for; and the Pilsener at the Kaiserhof Restaurant in the Goetheplatz is equally good. One has to sample several glasses of each before one can definitely make up one's mind as to which is the best.

Düsseldorf

The best restaurant in Düsseldorf is that of the Park Hotel on the Corneliusplatz. It is one of the best on the Rhine, and was opened in April 1902 on the occasion of the Düsseldorf Exhibition; it is a fine building, and has pretty grounds and ornamental water adjoining it. It is frequented by the highest German nobility, but yet its prices are moderate.

Luncheons are served at 3 marks, dinners at 5 marks. Suppers for 3 marks are served at *prix fixe*, or one can order *à la carte*. The Moselle wines are exceptionally good. There is an American bar in the hotel. The restaurant, handsomely decorated in the style of Louis XIV., is opposite the Opera House and overlooks the Hofgärten.

It has no specialities in the way of food beyond the usual German and French dishes.

At the Thürnagel Restaurant, also in the Corneliusplatz, you are likely to find the artistic colony in session. The restaurant dates back to the year 1858. There is a good collection of wine in the cellars, and a word may be said in favour of its cookery.

The Rhine Valley

The Rhine valley is not a happy hunting ground for the gourmet. Cologne has its picturesque Gurzenich in which is a restaurant; its inhabitants eat their oysters in the saloon in the Kleine Bugenstrasse, part of a restaurant there; and there are restaurants in the Marienburg and in the Stadt garden, and the Flora and Zoological Gardens. At every little town on either bank there are one or more taverns with a view where the usual atrocities which pass as food in provincial Germany are to be obtained, good beer, and generally excellent wine made from the vineyards on the mountain side. Now and again some restaurant-keeper has a little pool of fresh water in front of his house, and one can select one's particular fish to be cooked for breakfast. The wines of the district are far better than its food.

Rudesheim, Geisenheim, Schloss Johannisberg, the Steinberg Abbey above Hattenheim, are of course household words, and the man who said that travelling along the Rhine was like reading a restaurant wine-list had some justification for his Philistine speech. One does not expect to discover the real Steinberg Cabinet in a village inn, and the Johannisberg generally found in every hotel in Rhineland is a very inferior wine to that of the Schloss, and is grown in the vineyards round Dorf Johannisberg. I have memories of excellent bottles of wine at the Ress at Hattenheim, and at the Engel at Erbach; but the fact that I was making a walking tour may have added to the delight of the draughts. The Marcobrunn vineyards lie between Hattenheim and Erbach. The Hôtel Victoria at Bingen has its own vineyards and makes a capital wine; and in the valley of the river below Bingen almost every little town and hill—Lorch, Boppard, Horcheim, and the Kreuzberg—has its own particular brand, generally excellent. Assmanhausen, which gives such an excellent red wine, is on the opposite bank to Bingen and a little below it. The Rhine boats have a very good assortment of wines on board, but it is wise to run the finger a little way down the list before ordering your bottle, for the very cheapest wines on the Rhine are, as is usual in all countries, of the thinnest description. Most of the British doctors on the Continent make the greater part of their living by attending their fellow-countrymen who drink everywhere anything that is given them free, and who hold that the *vin du pays* must be drinkable because it *is* the wine of the country. Our compatriots often swallow the throat-cutting stuff which the farm labourers and stable hands drink, sooner than pay a little extra money for the sound wine of the district. The foreigner who came to Great Britain and drank our cheapest ale and rawest whisky would go away with a poor impression of the liquors of *our* country. Drink the wine of the district where they make good wine, but do not grudge the extra shilling which makes all the difference in quality. The dinners and lunches on the big express Rhine steamers are a scramble for food; but on some of the smaller and slower boats, where the caterer has fewer passengers to feed, the meals are often very good. I have a kindly memory of an old head steward, a fatherly old gentleman in a silk cap shaped somewhat like an accordion, who provided the meals on a leisurely steamer which pottered up the Rhine, stopping at every village. He gave us local delicacies, took an interest in our appetites, and his cookery, though distinctively German, was also very good. In a land where all the big hotels fill once a day and empty once a day, and where the meals are in heavy-handed imitation of bourgeois French cookery, that old man with his stews and roasts, and pickles, veal, and pork, sausages big and sausages small, strange cheeses, and Delikatessen of all kinds was a good man to meet.

German "Cure" Places

First of course amongst the places in Germany where men and women mend their constitutions and enjoy themselves at the same time comes

Homburg

The "Homburg Dinner" has become a household word, meaning that a certain number of men and women agree to dine together at one of the hotels, each one paying his or her own share in the expenses. During the past two years, owing to the desire to spend money shown by some millionaires, British and American, who are not happy unless they are giving expensive dinners every night with a score of guests, this pretty old custom seems likely now to die out. In no German town are there better hotels than at Homburg, and one dines on a warm day in very pleasant surroundings, for Ritter's has its world-famous terrace, and some of the other hotels have very delightful open-air restaurants in their gardens. Simplicity, good plain food well cooked, is insisted on by the doctors at Homburg, and therefore a typical Homburg dinner is a very small affair compared to German feasts over which the doctors do not have control. This is a dinner of the day at Ritter's, taken haphazard from a little pile of menus, and it may be accepted as a typical Homburg dinner:—

Potage Crécy au Riz.
Truite de Lac. Sce. Genevoise. Pommes Natures.
Longe de Veau à la Hongroise.

Petits pois au Jambon.
Chapons de Châlons rôtis.
Salade and Compots. Pêches à la Cardinal.
Fruits. Dessert.

The hotels at Homburg are always quite full in the season. No hotel-keeper puts any pressure on his guests to dine at his hotel, and you may have your bedroom in one hotel and dine at another every night of your life so far as the proprietors care. All those who have the luck to be made members of the Golf Club take tea there, and eat cake such as is only to be found at school-treats in England. The restaurant at the Kurhaus goes up and down in public favour. Everybody goes to its terrace in the evening, and fashion at the present time has, I believe, ordained that on one particular day of the week it is "smart" to dine there. If the restaurant remains as excellently catered for as it was when I last visited Homburg, it is well worth including in the round of dinners.

WIESBADEN

At Wiesbaden you generally dine where you sleep, in your hotel. I myself have generally stayed at the Kaiser Hof, because I like to eat my supper on its creeper-hung terrace and look across the broad valley to the Taunus hill; but there are half-a-dozen hotels in the town, the Nassauer Hof in particular, which many people consider the best hotel in Germany, having capital restaurants, serving *table-d'hôte* meals, attached to them. The Rose has a little terrace, looking on to the gardens, which is a pleasant supping-place. The old Kurhaus, a tumble-down building, is disappearing or has disappeared, and a new and gorgeous building is to take its place. The restaurant at the old Kurhaus always had a good reputation, and to eat one's evening meal, for every one sups and does not dine, at one of its little tables under the trees, looking at the lake beneath the moonshine and listening to the band, was one of the pleasures of

Wiesbaden. It was fairly cheap, and I thought the food well cooked, and served as hot as one could expect it in the open air. I have little doubt that the new restaurant will carry on the pleasant ways of the old one. The proprietor is Herr Ruthe, who is caterer to several crowned heads, and who is always on the spot and delighted to be consulted as to the dishes to be ordered for a dinner.

The wine-house, the Rathskeller, is one of the sights of the place. Therein are quaint frescoes and furniture, there the usual German food is obtainable, and *you* have a choice of German wines such as is obtainable in few other wine-drinking places in Germany.

Any one who likes the open tarts of apple and other fruits—a rather sticky delicacy it always seems to me—can eat them at ease of an afternoon looking at the beautiful view from the Neroberg or watching the Rhine from under the trees of the hotel gardens at Biebrich.

Baden-Baden

The first-class hotels in Baden-Baden are so well catered for that few people wander abroad to take their food, but the restaurant of the Conversation Haus is a good one. The little restaurant, with a shady terrace on the Alte-Schloss Hohenbaden, has achieved celebrity for its trout *au bleu* and good cookery, and the marvellous view over the Rhine valley makes it a notable little place. There are many refreshment-places on the roads along which the patients take their walks, but as milk is the staple nourishment sold, they hardly find a place in a guide for gourmets. The wines of the Duchy, both red and white, are excellent.

Ems

Ems has a restaurant in the Kursaal, near which the band plays in the evening, said to be fairly good; and there is a restaurant close to the Baderlei, the cliff of rock crowned by a tower, and another on the summit of the Malberg, the hill up which the wire-rope railway runs; but I have only meagre information as to whether the food obtainable at them is good, bad, or indifferent.

Aachen (Aix-la-Chapelle)

Henrion's Grand Hotel is the favourite dining-place of the Anglo-Saxon colony in Aachen. M. Intra, the proprietor, lays himself out to attract the English. The German civil servants and the doctors have a club-table at which they dine, and they exact fines from the members of their club for drinking wine which costs more than a certain price, etc., etc., these fines being collected in a box and saved until they make a sum large enough to pay for a special dinner. Every member of this club is required to leave in his will a money legacy to the club to be expended in wine drunk to his memory. There are two *table-d'hôte* meals at 1.30 and at 7 P.M. At the first the dishes are cooked according to the German cuisine, at the second according to the French. Suppers are served in the restaurant at any hour.

Lennertz's restaurant and oyster-saloon in the Klostergasse is a curious, low-ceilinged, old-fashioned house which, before Henrion's came into favour, had most of the British patronage. Its cooking is excellent, and the German Hausfraus used to be sent to Lennertz's to study for their noble calling. The *carte de jour* has not many dishes on it. Everything has to be ordered *à la carte*, though the prices are reasonable, and it is possible to make a bargain that a dinner shall be given for a fixed price. The *Omelettes Soufflées* are a speciality of the house. The fish used at Lennertz's comes from Ostend, and the Dutch oysters are excellent.

A restaurant opposite the theatre has good cookery but is expensive.

Henry, who presides over the Anglo-American bar in the Kaiser Passage, is an excellent cook and turns out wonderful dishes with the aid of a chafing-dish. He learned his cookery at the Waldorf, and at the Grand, in Paris. His partner, Charlie, is of the Café de Paris, Monte Carlo.

Another American bar where food is obtainable is in the Grand Monarque Hotel.

The Alt-Bayern in Wirischsbongardstrasse is the beer-house which is most to be recommended; and the Germania, in Friedrich-Williamplatz, is celebrated for its coffee.

KIEL

Kiel Harbour is as beautiful and picturesque a spot as one can well imagine. The approach to it from the Elbe by the Kaiser Wilhelm Canal— 52 miles long, 70 yards broad, and about 30 feet deep, with pretty banks on either side, is part of the river Eider. It is lighted along its entire length with electric lamps, and constitutes as pleasant a waterway as one can desire.

The hotels and restaurants are neither numerous nor *récherché*, and, with the exception of the sailor's rendezvous, are mostly closed during the winter. The Seebadeanstalt is about the best restaurant; it was built by Herr Krupp and is managed by an Englishman. Above it are the fine rooms of the Imperial Yacht Club. These, during the regatta week, which generally takes place at the end of June, are crowded with yachtsmen of all nationalities, to whom the Kaiser dispenses most gracious hospitality. When the extensive anchorage, surrounded by green and wooded hills, is full of every description of yacht, foremost among which is the *Hohenzollern* and many German battleships, it forms a scene at once impressive and gay. One can hardly blame the Germans for annexing it, however galling its annexation by Germany must have been to its former owners.

The Hôtel Germania has a very fair restaurant attached to it.

The Rathskeller is well-conducted, and was built by the municipal authorities.

The Weinstuben, Paul Fritz, is a good refreshment-place, but is mostly frequented by the students and officers.

The Seegarten is a pretty little place overlooking the harbour, where German beer is the principal article of commerce.

At the Münchener Bürgerbrau the beer is good but the surroundings dismal.

Hamburg

At Hamburg is to be found Pfordte's Restaurant, which has gained a European reputation; indeed, it is spoken of as the "Paillard's of North Germany." The following description of the restaurant is from the pen of an English *habitué* of the house:—

Pfordte's Restaurant, which dates back to the year 1828, was originally one of the numerous Kellers or cellars which are situated in many of the basements of the houses near the Alster and Bourse at Hamburg. Their function is to provide luncheons, dinners, or suppers, and their chief *spécialités* are oysters, lobsters, other shell-fish, game, and truffles. They are much frequented by business men for luncheon, and by playgoers for supper after the theatre.

Mr. Wilkins was the first proprietor, and in 1842 it was in the hands of a company. In 1860 Pfordte, who had become director of this Keller, aimed at higher things. Being a good organiser and administrator, he eventually moved the Keller to the street that runs from the Alster Dam to the Rathaus gardens, and there, at the corner of the gardens, established a restaurant which is one of the best in the world.

Pfordte is a man of small stature but of most courteous and polished manners, and is no exception to the general rule that small men have usually great brains. His restaurant is *facile princeps* of all the houses of entertainment at Hamburg where riches abound, and where good cheer is scientifically appreciated. Entering the establishment from the street, you find yourself in a fair-sized hall, where a deferential servant in livery is prompt to relieve men of their overcoats and ladies of their wraps.

On the left, a large folding-door gives entrance to three public rooms *en suite* which look out on the Rathaus gardens, and are furnished with small tables—some for two, some for four, some for six persons. Here a most excellent dinner or luncheon can be obtained at short notice. The service is capital. The waiters are German, but appear to be conversant with every tongue in the world. All sorts and conditions of men have to visit Hamburg, the great centre of maritime commerce in Germany. All seem to be able at Pfordte's to give orders in their own language, and find themselves understood. English seems as much spoken here as German.

On the right of the entrance-hall, a fine staircase leads to the first floor, where are rooms for private parties of any number, from two to a hundred. Hardly any important public dinner is held at Hamburg which does not take place at Pfordte's. The cuisine is perfect. The menus are original, the wines are of the best. If you are at Hamburg in the proper season, do not fail at Pfordte's to order oysters, trout from the hill streams, partridge with apricots, and *truffes en serviette*.

To the above there is but little to add except that there is a certain cosiness about Pfordte's, a sense of personal supervision, which is difficult to define but which everybody who dines there feels and appreciates. One Londoner put it thus, referring to the little rooms, "It's what Kettner's ought to be." I append a menu of a dinner of the day at Pfordte's, there being a choice of four or five dishes in each course. The charge is 6 marks. This bill of fare is by no means an exceptionally good one. Indeed it is below the average rather than above. The "English" adjective to the celery is used to distinguish it from celleriac or "Dutch" celery, which is largely used in salads in North Germany. The *Junger Puter* is a very little turkey poult. It is to the turkey what the *poussin* is to the fowl:—

Potage à la Stuart.
Potage crème d'orge à la Viennoise.
Potage purée de concombres au cerfeuil.

Consommé Xavier.
Filets von Seezungen (soles) à la Joinville.
Steinbutt (turbot) sauce moscovite.
Rheinlachs kalt, sauce mayonnaise.
Bœuf braisé à l'alsacienne.
Rehbrücken (venison) à la Conti.
Lammviertel à la Provençale.
Roast-beef à la Clamart.
Artischoken sauce hollandaise.
Salat braisirt mit jungen Erbsen.
Engl. Sellerie mit Mark.
Junge Flageolets à la Maître.
Spanishe Pfefferschoten farcirt.
Junge Ente (duckling).
Rebhuhn (partridge).
Junge Puter.
Escarolle-Salat mit Tomaten.
Erdbeer-Eiscrème panaché Fruchttorte.
Kasé.

Dress clothes are not *de rigueur* when dining at Pfordte's. Bordeaux wines are a speciality of the house, as indeed they are in every good restaurant in Hamburg and Bremen, better claret being found in those cities than anywhere else outside France that I know of. There is a celebrated picture in Pfordte's hall which has a story attached to it. The painter wished to give a dinner to his club friends, and consulted Pfordte as to the price. Pfordte said that he would supply the dinner, and that the artist afterwards should paint him a picture. The dinner was given to the entire club, and was said to have been the best dinner ever served in Germany: the artist showed his appreciation of it by painting a masterpiece.

This is a specimen of one of Pfordte's dinners of ceremony:—

Nectar old sherry.	Natives.
	Astrachan Caviar.
1894 *Louis Roederer grand vin sec.*	Potage Malmesbury.
	Truffes du Périgord à la Savarin.
1876 *Geisenheimer Hothenberg-*	Saiblinge aus dem Königssee.
Auslese.	Bayrische Sauce.
1889 *Chât. Dauzac Labarde*	Engl. Hammebrücken à la
(Tischwein).	Courdomage.
1878 *Chât. Marquis de Therme.*	Côtelettes de Macassins à la
	Montalembert.
1869 *Clos St-Hobert.*	Suprême von Strassburger
	Gänselebern in Madeira.
	Crème de Chicorées aux pointes
	d'asperges vertes.
	Fonds d'artichauts à la St-Charles.
1874 *Chât. Larose Schloss-Olbzug.*	Enten von Rouen.
	Salade à la Française.
Moet and Chandon Crémant blanc.	Pouding glacé à la Jules Lecomte.
	Dessert.

At the Zoological Gardens there is a good restaurant where one dines in a balcony overlooking the beer-garden, in which a military band plays.

The oyster-cellars of Hamburg are noted for their excellent lunches. *Bouillon*, cutlets, steaks, caviar, lachs, and other viands are served, and English "porter," generally Combe's stout, is much drunk. Another British production, "Chester" cheese, which is red Cheshire, is much in demand. At supper in these cellars, and also in Berlin, caviar is much in demand, the small black Baltic variety, not the Russian, which is lighter in colour and larger in grain. A large pot of it is put on the table in a bowl of ice, and your Hamburger, who is a good judge of victuals as he is of drink, makes his supper of it.

The Rathskeller of Hamburg is in the modern Rathhaus, and is finely decorated in "Alt-deutsch" style with frescoes and paintings by well-known artists.

In the summer gardens down the Elbe, good wines are to be obtained; and at the Fährhaus at Blauenesse.

The Alster Café is very beautifully situated. It has three tiers of rooms, and from its balconies one can look either landward or on to the river, which at night, with the lights reflected in its water, is very beautiful. The rooms of the café are decorated in the style of the seventeenth century.

CHAPTER VII

BERLIN

Up-to-date restaurants—Supping-places—Military cafés—Night restaurants.

Twenty years ago Berlin had no restaurant worthy of the name, now of course they are plentiful; in many instances, however, showy paintings, bad gilding, and heavy decorations seem to atone with a certain class of the public for inferior *matériel* and mediocre cookery.

The Monopole part of the Hôtel-Restaurant L. Schaurté is first-rate, and the set dinner for the price is as good as one could get anywhere. I append an everyday menu which, for 5 marks, ought to satisfy the most exacting customer. The second soup is a *Consommé* with *quenelles*. The fish dishes are *Sole Normande* and *Turbot au Gratin*.

MENU.

From 2 P.M. to 9 P.M.

Häringfilet nach Daube.
Mulligatawny-Suppe.
Kraftbrühe mit Einlage.
Seezungenfilet auf normännische Art.
Steinbutt in Muscheln gratiniert.
Eng. Roast-beef.

Yorker Schinken in Burgunder.
Spinat.
Homard de Norvège. Sauce Ravigotte.
Französ. Poularde.
Fasan.
Salat Compot.
Sellerie.
Fürst Pückler Bombe.
Käse. Früchte.
Nachtisch.

Estimated cost of two dinners at the Restaurant Schaurté (Monopole):—

	M. Pfgs.		M. Pfgs.
Dinner	5 00	Dinner	5 00
1/2 Pontet Canet (1890)	7 00	1/2 Roederer (1893 Reserve for England)	8 75
Coffee	60	1 Cognac (1860)	75
Cognac	60	Coffee	60
	13 20		15 10

If you drink no wine with the above repast, you are charged 6 marks for the dinner instead of 5. The wine charges are rather expensive, otherwise there is no fault to be found. This restaurant is a fashionable place at which to sup.

The Bristol Restaurant, attached to the hotel of that name, is also one of the best and answers, on a reduced scale, to the Carlton Restaurant in London; you get as good a dinner at the Bristol as you can wish to have, especially if you interview Mons. Maxim (who was for a time in London) the *maître-d'hôtel*, a proceeding which will ensure your being well cared for.

In fact with regard to most restaurants, it is always better, in Berlin as elsewhere in the world, if you have time or happen to be passing that way, to look in wherever you may have settled to dine, choose your table, and see what they propose to give you. It simplifies and expedites matters on arriving, especially if you are going on to some entertainment and have not much time to spare.

Borchard's, in the Französischerstrasse, is a capital place to drop in to lunch, as there is a cold buffet there with every sort of Delikatesse. You can get a very good dinner there, and the wines are of excellent quality. The attachés of the British Embassy patronise it, and it is to the Bristol in Berlin what Claridge's is to the Carlton in London.

The Hôtel de Rome has an excellent restaurant, and many dinners of ceremony are given there. This is the menu, headed by the motto, "The Tubercle Bacillus will federate the World," of a dinner given at the Berlin by a distinguished British physician to some of his German colleagues of the great Congress:—

Hors-d'œuvre.
Consommé Sévigné.
Potage Oxtail.
Sole à la Bordelaise.
Filet de bœuf à la Moderne.
Côtelettes de Foies gras aux Truffes.
Faisan Rôti.
Compote Salade.
Asperges en branches.
Prince Pückler.
Fromage.
Fruits.

The Palast Hotel and restaurant, at the corner of the Potsdamerplatz, and the Savoy in the Friedrichstrasse are also excellent.

The Hiller and the Dressel, in the Unter den Linden, are bright, pleasant, and good restaurants. Dressel gives an excellent lunch for 2.50 and dinners for 3 marks or 5. This is a sample lunch:—

Bouillon in Tassen.
Eier Skobeleff.
Seezunge gebacken, Sauce Tartare.
Kalbskopf aux Champignons.
Mutton Chops.
Pfirsich nach Condé.
Käse.

The English bar in the Passage is a grill-room and restaurant, and ladies can lunch there, though the sporting British element is rather too prominent. In the evening it is frequented by the theatrical world and is practically open all night. One can enjoy a peaceable supper there without having to pay the bill and leave shortly after one has sat down, as is the custom in England.

Kempinsky's, in the Leipzigerstrasse, a very popular restaurant and always crowded, rather corresponds to Scott's in the Haymarket. Here you get very good oysters (when in season) and excellent Holstein crayfish, lobsters, etc. The cook at this restaurant has an excellent manner of cooking lobsters, called *Homard chaud au beurre truffé*. It consists of chopped truffles worked up into best fresh butter rolled out, and then laid on the hot lobster.

I subjoin a menu, in order to show the moderate charge for an extremely well-cooked dinner. As a rule a portion of any dish on the bill of fare costs M. 1.25.

MENU.

Hors-d'œuvre.
Consommé double à la Moelle.
Homard chaud au Beurre Truffé.

Escaloppes de Veau.
Choux de Bruxelles.
Faisan Rôti.
Salade.
Fromage, Céleri.
Café, Cigare.
1 Bottle German Champagne.

For two people, including the champagne, the total came to 12 marks 75 = 12s. 9d.

As to the German champagne, "Sect," as it is called, they are now making very pleasant light wines of this character in the country at very reasonable prices. They are excellent of their sort, though they are rarely kept long enough in the cellar, and I should certainly advise their being tried, in preference to paying heavily for *soi-disant* French brands which in Germany are of very doubtful origin. "Herb" does not guarantee what we understand by "dry."

If you wish to sample German dishes well and inexpensively, you could not do better than go to the Rüdesheimer in the Friedrichstrasse. The house can provide you with an excellent bottle of Rhine wine, having a special celebrity for this.

The Reichshof, in the Wilhelmstrasse, is a café of a more Bohemian description. It is most frequented towards the evening and for suppers after the theatres; usually a first-class but very noisy band is engaged there. It is also a good hotel. It is next door to the British Embassy.

There are also two cafés in which the military element predominates, one might almost say exclusively. These are Topfer's and the Prinz Wilhelm, both in the Dorotheenstrasse. Here the officers usually lunch and make a general rendezvous, often bringing their wives.

There are, of course, plenty of suburban cafés open in the summer, but they are more refreshment establishments, and appeal rather to the general public than to the higher class; they are opened or closed according to the seasons.

Bauer's, in Unter den Linden, is also a well-known café, and is much frequented by the Berliners; it is, however, more of the refreshment saloon class, and is patronised by a large newspaper-reading public, from the fact that there are few of the leading publications in all languages that you would fail to find here. This café has become a general rendezvous in the afternoon and evening, and everything supplied there is of the best quality. The walls are decorated with paintings by the eminent German artists of thirty years ago. Upstairs, between 5 and 6 P.M., one sees many of the people of the world of the theatres and music halls.

At Ewest, just off the Friedrichstrasse, there are two or three little quiet dining-rooms. The management is not anxious to find accommodation for any except old customers, but the best wine in Berlin is to be obtained there.

The Kaiserkeller, with its rooms decorated splendidly in various styles, one after the model of the Lübeck Schiffergesellschaft, and others after other famous German rooms, is one of the sights of Berlin. It retains an army of cooks and its wine-list is a wonderful one.

If you wish to see the rowdy student life of Berlin, the Bohemian festivity which corresponds to the life of Paris in the *cabarets* of Montmartre, and if you speak German, go to the Bauernschänke, which has obtained a celebrity for the violence and rudeness of its proprietor, who, as Lisbonne and Bruant used to, and Alexander does in the *cabarets* of the City of Light, insults his customers to the uttermost and turns out any one who objects. Die Räuberhohle is an inferior imitation of Die Bauernschänke.

A noted night restaurant is Der Zum Weissen Rössl, in which each room is decorated to represent some typical street in Berlin. This is a hostel much frequented by artists.

CHAPTER VIII

SWITZERLAND

Lucerne—Basle—Bern—Geneva—Davos Platz.

Switzerland is a country of hotels and not of restaurants. In most of the big towns the hotels have restaurants attached to them, and in some of these a dinner ordered *à la carte* is just as well cooked as in a good French restaurant, and served as well; in other restaurants attached to good hotels the *table-d'hôte* dinner is served at separate tables at any time between certain hours, and this is the custom of most of the restaurants in most of the better class of hotels. There is in every little mountain-hotel a restaurant; but this is generally used only by invalids, or very proud persons, or mountaineers coming back late from a climb. There is no country in which the gourmet has to adapt himself so much to circumstances and in which he does it, thanks to exercise and mountain air, with such a Chesterfieldian grace. I have seen the man who, at the restaurants of the Schweitzerhof or National at Lucerne, ate a perfectly cooked little meal which he had ordered *à la carte* on the day of his arrival in Switzerland, and who was hoping to find something to grumble at, sitting in peace two days later eating the *table-d'hôte* meal at a little table in the restaurant of one of the hotels at Lauzanne or Vevey, Montreux or Territet, after a walk along the lake side or up the mountain to Caux, and four days after one at a long table at Zermatt or the Riffel Alp, talking quite happily to perfect strangers on either side of him and eating the menu through from end to end, more conscious of the splendid appetite a day on the glaciers had given him than of what he is eating. Switzerland entirely demoralises the judgment of a gourmet, for its mountain air gives it undue advantages over most other countries, and an abundant appetite has a way of paralysing all the finer critical faculties.

At one period all hotels in Switzerland were "run" on one simple, cheap, easy plan. There were meals at certain hours, there was a table in the big room for the English, another for the Germans, and another for mixed nationalities. If any one came late for a meal, so much the worse for him or her, for they had to begin at the course which was then going round. If travellers appeared when dinner was half over, they had to wait till it was quite finished; and then, as a favour, the *maître-d'hôtel* would instruct a waiter to ask the cook to send the late comers in something to eat, which was generally some of the relics of the just-completed feast, the odours of which still hung about the great empty dining-hall.

I fancy that it is a matter of history that M. Ritz, who has since become the Napoleon of hotels, coming as manager to the National at Lucerne and finding this system in practice, put an end to it at once and started the restaurant there, which was and is quite first class. Whether some one else was making history at the Schweitzerhof at the same time in the same way I do not know, but the two hotels have run neck and neck in the excellence of their restaurants, and not only are they first rate, but, as is always the case, the average of the cooking at the other hotels has gone up in sympathy, as the doctors would say, with the two leading caravanserais, and one usually finds that any one who has stayed at Lucerne has a good word to say for his hotel. I was once at Lucerne during race week, and was doubtful whether I should find a room vacant at either of the hotels I usually stay at. A charming old priest, who was a fellow-voyager, suggested to me that I should come to a little hotel hard by the river; and there, though the room I was given was of the very old continental pattern, the dinner my friend ordered for himself and me was quite excellent. I have breakfasted at the buffet at the station and found it very clean, and the simple food was well cooked. There is a restaurant at the Kursaal, but I have never had occasion to breakfast or dine there.

In Northern Switzerland some of the towns have restaurants which are not attached to hotels, and Basle has quite a number of them, though the interest attaching to most of them is due to the quaintness of the buildings they are in or the fine view to be obtained from them rather than from any particular excellence of cookery or any surprisingly good cellar. The restaurant in the Kunsthalle, for instance, is ornamented by some good wall paintings; and by the old bridge there is a restaurant with a pleasant terrace overlooking the river. There is a good cellar at the Schutzenhaus, and there is music and a pretty garden as an attraction to take visitors out to the Summer Casino.

Of the Bern restaurants much the same is to be said as of the Basle ones. Historical paintings are thought more of than the cook's department. The Kornhauskeller, in the basement of the Kornhaus, is a curious place and worth a visit for a meal. At the Schauzli, on a rise opposite the town, from the terrace of which there is a splendid view and where there is a summer theatre, there is a café-restaurant, and another on the Garten, a hill whence another fine view is obtainable.

Geneva, for its size and importance, is the worst catered for capital in Europe. Outside the hotel restaurants, none of which have attained any special celebrity, there are but few restaurants, and those not of any conspicuous merit. There is a restaurant in the noisy Kursaal, and two in the Rue de Rhone, and most of the cafés on the Grand Quai are feeding-places as well; but I never ate a dinner yet in Geneva—and I have known the place man and boy, as they say in nautical melodrama, for thirty-five years—that was worth remembering; and though the trout are as palatable as they were when Cambacérès used to import them to France for his suppers, I have never tasted the *Ombre Chevalier* of which Hayward wrote appreciatively. There are two little out-of-door restaurants which are amusing to breakfast at during the summer. One is in the Jardin Anglais and the other in the Jardin des Bastions. At each a cheap *table-*

d'hôte meal is served at little tables. There is also a restaurant in the Park des Eaux Vives.

On the borders of the Lake of Geneva there are many good hotels, though some of the best of them pick and choose their visitors, and writing beforehand does not mean that a room will be found for a bachelor who only intends to stay a few days. The better the hotel the better the restaurant, and if the haughty hotel porter at the station says "No" very courteously when you look appealingly at him and ask if a room has been kept for you, the only way is to try the next on your list. Fresh-water fish, fruit, cheese, honey, are all excellent by the lake, and the wines of the Rhone valley are some of them excellent. At Lauzanne, Vevey, Montreux, Territet, the wines of the country are well worth tasting, for in the valley above Villeneuve there are a dozen vineyards each producing an excellent wine; and the vines imported from the Rhine valley, from the Bordeaux and Burgundy districts, give wine which is excellent to drink and curious as well, when the history of the vine is known. Always ask what the local cheese is. There are varieties of all kinds, and they afford a change from the eternal slab of Gruyère.

Of course Switzerland has its surprises like every other country, and one does not expect to find an ex-head *chef* of Claridge's running a little restaurant by a lake in the Swiss mountains. Mr. Elsener, who is this benefactor to humanity, was the head of the catering department at the Imperial Institute when a very praiseworthy effort was made to make a smart dining place in the arid waste called a garden in the centre of the buildings; and he also catered for the Coldstream Guards, so that he started business with a good *clientèle*. As a sample of what can be done on the mountain heights, I give the menu of one of the dinners served by Elsener at the restaurant Villa Fortuna:—

Huîtres d'Ostende.
Consommé Riche.
Filet de Sole au Vin Blanc.

Tournedos à l'Othello.
Petits Pois. Pommes paille.
Vol-au-vent à la Banquier.
Aspic de foie gras en belle vue.
Melons Glacé Vénitienne.
Petit Fours.
Omelette à la Madras.
Petit Soufflé au Parmesan.
Dessert.

N.N.-D.

CHAPTER IX

ITALY

Italian cookery and wines—Turin—Milan—Genoa—Venice—Bologna—Spezzia—Florence—Pisa—Leghorn—Rome—Naples—Palermo.

Italian Cookery

There is no cookery in Europe so often maligned without cause as that of Italy. People who are not sure of their facts often dismiss it contemptuously as being "all garlic and oil," whereas very little oil is used except at Genoa, where oil, and very good oil as a rule, takes the place of butter, and no more garlic than is necessary to give a slight flavour to the dishes in which it plays a part. An Italian cook frys better than one of any other nationality. In the north very good meat is obtainable, the boiled beef of Turin being almost equal to our own Silverside. Farther and farther south, as the climate becomes hotter, the meat becomes less and less the food of the people, various dishes of paste and fish taking its place, and as a compensation the fruit and the wine become more delicious. The fowls and figs of Tuscany, the white truffles of Piedmont, the artichokes of Rome, the walnuts and grapes of Sorrento, might well stir a gourmet to poetic flights. The Italians are very fond of their *Risotto*, the rice which they eat with various seasonings,—with sauce, with butter, and with more elaborate preparations. They also eat their *Paste asciutte* in various forms. It is *Maccheroni* generally in Naples, *Spagetti* in Rome, *Trinetti* in Genoa. *Alla Siciliana* and *con Vongole* are but two of the many ways of seasoning the *Spagetti*. Again, the delicate little envelopes of paste containing forcemeat of some kind or another change their names according to their contents and the town they are made in. They are *Ravioli* both at Genoa and Florence, but at Bologna they are *Capeletti*, and at Turin *Agnolotti*. *Perpadelle*, another pasta dish with a little difference of seasoning, becomes *Tettachine* when the venue changes from Bologna to Rome.

There are many minor differences in the components of similarly named dishes at different towns; the *Minestrone* of Milan and Genoa differ, and so does the *Fritto Misto* of Rome and Turin. I fancy that, as a compensation, only an expert could tell the difference between the soups *di Vongole* at Naples, *di Dattero* at Spezzia, and *di Peoci* at Venice.

The "Zabajone" the sweet, frothing drink beaten up with eggs and sugar, is made differently in different towns. At Milan and Turin Marsala and brandy are used in it; at Venice Cyprus wine is the foundation; and elsewhere three wines are used. It is a splendidly sustaining drink, whether drunk hot or iced, and Italian doctors order it in cases of depression, and it might well find a place in the household recipes of English and American households. The wines of the various towns I have noted in writing of them. "Vino nostrano" or "del paese" brings from the waiter his list of the local juice of the grape, and the wine of the district is the wine to drink. Roughly speaking, the red wine is the best throughout Italy, the white of Bologna and the Veneto being the exceptions. Finally, do not be alarmed if at a *trattoria* a waiter puts before you a huge flask of wine. It has been weighed before it is brought to you. It will be weighed when the waiter takes it away after you have finished, and what you have drunk, plus the great gulp the waiter is sure to take if he gets a chance, is what you will be charged for.

The Anglo-Saxon travelling in Italy is likely to strike Turin, or Milan, or Genoa as his first big town, according to the route he has chosen, and those are therefore the three towns the capabilities of which I shall first try to describe.

Turin

You will be fed well enough at your hotel whether you are at the Grand, or Kraft's, or the Trombetta, but if you want to test the cookery of the town I should suggest a visit to the Ristorante della Meridiana, which is in the Via Santa Theresa, the street which joins the Piazza Solferino and San Carlo; or to the Ristorante del Cambio, which is in the Piazza Carignano, where stands a marble statue of a philosopher and which has a couple of palaces as close neighbours. At these, or at the Lagrange and Nazionale, both in the Via Lagrange, you will get the dishes of Turin.

If you wish to commence with *hors-d'œuvre*, try the *Pepperoni*, which are large yellow or red chillies preserved in pressed grapes and served with oil and vinegar, salt and pepper. The *Grissini*, the little thin sticks of bread which are made in Turin and are famous for their digestible quality, will be by your plate. Next I should suggest the *Busecca*, though it is rather satisfying, being a thick soup of tripe and vegetables; and then must come a great delicacy, the trout from the Mount Cenis lake. For a meat course, if the boiled beef of the place, always excellent, is too serious an undertaking, or if the *Frittura Mista* is too light, let me recommend the *Rognone Trifolato*, veal kidney stewed in butter with tomatoes and other good things, including a little Marsala wine. The white Piedmontese truffles served as a salad, or with a hot sauce, must on no account be overlooked; nor the *Cardons*, the white thistle, served with the same sauce; nor indeed the *Zucchini Ripieni*, which are stuffed pumpkins; and some *Fonduta*, the cheese of the country, melted in butter and eggs and sprinkled with white truffles, will form a fitting end to your repast unless you feel inclined for the biscuits of Novara, or *Gianduiotti*, which are chocolates or nougat from Alba or Cremona where they make violins as well as sweets. You should drink the wine of the country, Barbera or Barolo, Nebiolo or

Freisa; and I expect, if you really persevere through half the dishes I have indicated, that you will be glad of a glass of Moscato with the fruit. Take your coffee at the Café Romano if you long for "local colour."

Milan

In the town of arcades, white marble, and veal cutlets I generally eat my breakfast at one of the window tables of the Biffi, from which one sees the wonderful crowd—well-groomed officers of the Bersaglieri, the pretty ladies, the wondering peasants—that goes through the great Galleria; but if there is no window table available, and the head waiter fails to understand why he should give a table retained for a constant patron to a bird of passage, I go to the Savini, also in the great arcade, where I think the food is rather better cooked, but which has not the same tempting outlook. In the evening, if it is a cold day, I dine at the Orlogio, at the corner of the great square, a restaurant which some men find fault with, but where I have always been well treated; but if the day is hot, I as often as not go to the Cova, near the Scala, where a band plays after dinner in the garden. Such is my usual round, with a night-cap at the Gambrinus if I have been to one of the theatres; but I am penitently aware that my circle is a small one, and I am told that I should take the De Albertis and the Isola Botta into my list. Wherever one dines and wherever one breakfasts there are certain Milanese dishes which one should order. The *Minestrone* soup is a dish which is not only found all Italy over but which is popular in Austria and on the French Riviera as well; but the *Minestrone alla Milanese*, with its wealth of vegetables and suspicion of Parmesan, is especially excellent. The *Risotto Milanese*, rice slightly *sauté* in butter, then boiled in capon broth, and finally seasoned with Parmesan and saffron, is one of the celebrated Milanese dishes, but the simpler methods of serving *Risotto, al sugo, al burro*, or *con fegatini* suit better those who do not like saffron; or better still is a very well-known dish of another town, *Risotto Certosino*, in which the rice is seasoned with a sauce of crayfish and garnished with their tails. Then come the various manners of cooking veal, the *Côtelette à la Milanese*, cutlets plunged in beaten eggs and fried in butter after being crumbed, and others stewed with a little red wine and flavoured with rosemary; and the *Côtelette alla Marsigliese*, of batter, then ham, then meat which, when fried, is one of the dishes of the populace on a feast-day. *Ossobuco*, a shin of veal cut into slices and stewed with a flavouring of lemon rind, is another veal dish; and so is the delicate *Fritto Picatto* of calf's brains, liver, and tiny slices of flesh. *Polpette à la Milanese* are forcemeat balls stewed. *Panettone* are the cakes of the city and are much eaten at Carnival time. Stracchino or Crescenza is a cheese much like the French *Brie*. Gorgonzola all the world knows well; and though Parmesan takes its name from that Duchess of Parma who introduced it into France, the best quality comes from Lodi, near Milan. Val Policella and Valle d'Inferno are the wines to drink.

Genoa

Genoa is a town of noise and bustle. The worst curse one Genoese can pronounce to another is "May the grass grow before your door." The Genoese restaurants have not the best reputation in the world for either cleanliness or quiet; but at the Concordia, in the Via Garibaldi, you will find a cool and pleasant garden; and at the Gottardo you will discover the Genoese cookery in all its oily perfection, for the important difference between the cuisine of Genoa and of every other Italian town is that all its dishes are prepared with olive oil instead of butter.

Of course Genoa has its own especial *Minestrone* soup flavoured with *Pesto*, a paste in which pounded basil, garlic, Sardinia cheese, and olive oil are used; and the fish dishes are *Stocafisso alla Genovese*, stock-fish stewed with tomatoes and sometimes with potatoes as well, and a fry of red mullet, and *Moscardini*, which are cuttle-fish, oblong in shape and redolent of musk. The tripe of Genoa is as celebrated as that of Caen, and the *Vitello Uccelletto*, little squares of veal *sauté* with fresh tomatoes in oil and red wine, is a very favourite dish. The *Ravioli* I have already written of. The *Faina* somewhat resembles Yorkshire pudding made with pease-powder and oil. *Funghi a Fungetto* are the wild red mushrooms stewed in oil with thyme and tomatoes, and *Meizanne* is a small, bitter egg-plant, only found on the Riviera, stuffed with a cheese paste and then fried. *Pasqualina* is an Easter pie. The figs of Genoa are excellent. The wines are those *delle cinque terre*, and in some of the cellars you will find them dating back sixty years or more.

Venice

The city on the lagoons is the next town to be considered, for Verona has scarcely a cuisine of its own, and Padua sends its best food to the Venetian market, and its Bagnoli wine as well. The Restaurant Quadri, on the north side of the Piazza of St. Mark, is one of the best-known restaurants in Europe, and it is not expensive, for one can breakfast there well enough for 4 francs.

A gourmet of my acquaintance thus describes a typical breakfast at the Quadri. "When you go to the restaurant do not be induced to go upstairs where the tourists are generally invited, but take a little table on the ground floor, where you can see all the piazza life, and begin with a *Vermouth Amaro*, in lieu of a "cocktail." For *hors-d'œuvre* have some small crabs, cold, mashed up with *Sauce Tartare*, and perhaps a slice or two of *Presciuto Crudo*, raw ham cut as thin as cigarette-paper. After this a steaming *Risotto*, with *Scampe*, somewhat resembling gigantic prawns. Some cutlets done in Bologna style, a thin slice of ham on top and hot Parmesan and grated white truffles and *Fegato alla Veneziana* complete the repast, except for a slice of Strachino cheese. A bottle of Val Policella is exactly suited to this kind of repast, and a glass of fine-champagne (De Luze) for yourself and of ruby-coloured Alkermes for the lady, if your wife accompanies you, makes a good ending. The *maître-d'hôtel*, who looks like a retired ambassador, will be interested in you directly he finds that you know how a man should breakfast."

The restaurant which comes next in order in popularity with visitors is the Bauer-Grunwald, in the Via Ventidue Marzo, which has a garden with seats in it; but this is a German house, and can scarcely claim to represent anything Venetian. The Capello Nero, in the Merceria, behind the Piazza of St. Mark, is thoroughly Venetian and unpretentious, and there you may obtain the real cookery of the town; and another such *trattoria* attached to an hotel is the Cavalletto, by the Ponte Cavalletto, close to the great square; but the Venetian cookery, it should be thoroughly understood, is not eaten in Parisian surroundings.

At the Florian Café, which in the summer keeps open all the night through, one gets the frothing *Zabajone* made so stiff that a spoon stands upright in it.

There are many *birrerie* in Venice, the Dreher being one frequented by the Italians.

The *Zuppa di Peoci* is a soup made from the little shell-fish called "peoci" in Venice, and appearing under other names at Spezzia and Naples, and so fond are the Venetians of it that they flavour their rice with sauce made from it and call it *Riso coi peoci*. *Baccala*, or salt-cod, and *Calamai*, little cuttle-fish or octopi, looking and tasting like fried strips of soft leather, are native dishes not to be recommended; but the *Anguille di Comacchio*, the great eels from Comacchio, grilled on the spit between bay leaves, or fried or stewed, are excellent. Another Venetian dish which I can strongly recommend is the *Fegato alla Veneziana*, calf liver cut into thin slices, fried with onions in butter, and flavoured with lemon juice. Stewed larks, with a pudding of Veronese flour, are satisfying, and a sausage from the neighbouring Treviso, which also gives its name to the *Radici di Treviso*, is much esteemed. The *Pucca baruca* is one of the big yellow pumpkins baked. The wines are, of course, those of the mainland, Conegliano from Treviso and Val Policella from Verona.

Bologna

"Bologna la grassa" does not belie its nick-name, and it is said that the matronly ladies, all over forty, who cook for the rotund priests, are the *cordons bleus* of Italy. The restaurant of the Hôtel Brun is the one where the passing Anglo-Saxon generally takes his meals and a chat with the proprietor, who is generally addressed as Frank, is entertaining, for he owns vineyards behind the town, which he is happy to show to any one interested in vine-culture, and he makes his wine after the French manner. The Hôtel d'Italie is more an Italian house, and the Stella d'Italia, in the Via Rizzoli, is the typical popular restaurant of the town. At the Albergo Roma, on the Via d'Azeglio, I have lunched on good food for a couple of francs.

The *Coppaletti* I have already referred to. The *Perpadelle col Ragout* are made of the same dough as the French *nouilles*, in narrow strips boiled and seasoned with minced meat and Parmesan cheese. Another variety of this *Perpadelle alla Bolognese* has minced ham as a seasoning. Then come the far-famed sausages, the great *Codeghino*, boiled and served with spinach or mashed potatoes; the large, ball-shaped *Mortadella*, which is sometimes eaten raw; and the stuffed foreleg of a pig, which is boiled and served with spinach and mashed potatoes and which is a dish the Bolognese "conveyed" from Verona.

The wines are San Giovese and Lambresco.

Spezzia

Not at Spezzia itself, but at Porto Venere on the promontory at the entrance to the bay, will the gourmet find the *Zuppa di Datteri*, which is the great delicacy of the gulf. The *dattero* is a shell-fish which in shape resembles a date stone. It has a very delicate taste, and is eaten stewed with tomatoes and served with a layer of toast. The little inn, Del Genio, is not too clean, but the landlord will tell you that Byron and Shelley made no complaints when they lived there and that they had a thorough appreciation of the dainty *datteri*. Byron is said to have written most of his *Corsair* in a grotto at Porto Venere, and Shelley was cast up drowned on the sand across the gulf.

Florence

If you wish to be aristocratic in Florence you will lunch at Capitani's in the Via Tornabuoni, and in the afternoon you will lounge about the street until it is time to drink tea and eat cake at Giacosa's, or Doney's, or the Albion, or Digerini's, and Marinari's venture, next door to the library, after which you will look in at Vieusseux's to see if there is any news a-foot. You will then have eaten a very fair lunch cooked *à la Française*, and will have met in the course of the afternoon all your fellow country-men and country-women resident in Florence. If, however, you want to sample Florentine cookery, you will fly from the splendours of the road which leads to the bridge of the Trinity and will try Mellini's in the Via Calzajoli, which runs from the Piazza della Signoria to that of the cathedral, where you will find both German and Italian dishes; or if you wish to test the native art, untouched by Teuton heaviness, go to La Toscana in the same street. There you will find comparative quiet, and you can be quite sure that the fish you order will be fresh, for it is sent daily direct from Leghorn, where the owner of La Toscana has a branch establishment.

At night the Gambrinus in one corner of the Piazza Vittorio Emmanuele rocks with sound, a band plays at intervals, and till long past midnight red and white wine and most indifferent cigarettes are called for by the revellers. This is hardly a place at which ladies would enjoy themselves, and still less should they be taken to Paoli's—where the young Florentines amuse themselves with good oysters and bad company until the small hours of the morning grow big—or to Picciolo's.

The Café la Rosa is a typical haunt of the submerged tenth, with a corrosive drink of its own.

There are not very many dishes distinctively Florentine. *Stracotto*, braised beef with tomatoes, is one of them; and *Fegatini di pollo*, giblets stewed in wine sauce, is another. The Tuscan fowls are especially esteemed, and are roasted before a wood fire; and there is a special Florentine salad of haricot beans generally served with caviar. The figs, of many kinds, are delicious, and *Presciutto con fichi*, fresh figs and ham, are eaten all over Tuscany. The chestnuts from the Appenines are the best flavoured in Italy. Chianti is the local wine.

The Aurora is the restaurant to be patronised at Fiësoli. It has a little garden whence there is a fine view.

Pisa

The Nettuno at Pisa is the old-fashioned Italian inn, and it used to be the restaurant patronised by the officers of the garrison, but for some reason they quarrelled with the proprietor and transferred their custom to the other Italian restaurant and inn, the Cervia.

Pisa prides itself on its puddings and confectionary. The *Pattona* and *Castagnacci*, both *alla Pisana*, are puddings made of chestnut flour and olive oil, and flavoured with fruit. *Schiacciata* are Easter cakes. In the afternoon, after a walk on the Lungarno, all the world of Pisa goes to Bazzeli, the pastry-cook's shop, and there you may find the elders of the town and the high officers of the garrison, talking over affairs of State while they demolish many little cakes.

Leghorn

An Englishman who knows his Leghorn thoroughly, writes thus:—

The restaurant of the Albergo Giappone is one of the most famous eating-houses in Tuscany. The kitchen is not merely Italian, it is wholly Tuscan, and the Tuscan kitchen in skilful hands appears to content both the gourmet and the gourmand. Affairs once brought a distinguished English gourmet on a brief visit to Leghorn, and accident (for its fame had not preceded him) took him to the Giappone. Instead of staying three days, he stayed three weeks, so that he might ring all the changes of that wonderful menu, and he has since publicly declared that the kitchen of the Giappone is one of the finest in Europe. The English visitor to Leghorn is a rarity, but all famous Italians have at some time or other eaten at the Giappone—Crispi, Zanardelli, Cavallotti, Benedetto Brin, Puccini, Mascagni, to mention only a few among many. The proprietor is the Cav. Pasquale Cianfanelli, known even on the London market for the excellence of his Tuscan wines.

The full Tuscan dinner does not follow in the order of fish, entrée, roast, *pièce de résistance*, and game, but of boiled (*lesso*), fried (*fritto*), stewed (*umido*) and roast (*arrosto*). The boiled may be beef; the fried, sweetbread; the stewed, fish; the roast, pigeon; but this order is always maintained, and the stranger's disappointment at there being no fish after the soup has only been equalled by his astonishment when it turns up in the fourth place. It is for this reason that the Tuscan bill of fare proves such a puzzle to the stranger with only a smattering of the language, for it is not made out under the headings of fish, entrées, joint, etc., but of *lessi, fritti, umidi,* and *arrosti*; and fish, for instance, will be found under all four headings. Famous dishes at the Giappone are *Spaghetti a sugo di carne* (gravy sauce), *Risotto* with white truffles, *Arselle* (a small shell-fish) *alla Marinara*, *Triglie* (red mullet) *alla Livornese*, *Fritto misto* (mixed fry), *Controfiletto con Maccheroni*, etc. The diner cannot do better than keep to the ordinary *vino da pasto*, and end with the delicious *caffè espresso* and a *Val d'Ema* (Tuscan Chartreuse), green or yellow. The best Tuscan mineral water is the *Acqua Litiosa di S. Marco* (from the province of Grosseto), and it deserves more than a merely local fame. If the traveller's flask is not already empty, let him try some of its contents with this water, and he will have a pleasant surprise.

Another excellent restaurant in Leghorn is that attached to the Hôtel d'Angleterre-Campari, owned by Signori De-Stefani and Clerici, the latter of whom was for a time in London, at the Albergo d'Italia. The cuisine is North Italian and French, and the traveller not thoroughly converted to the Tuscan table will find himself extremely well treated at the Hôtel Campari.

ROME

A man who loved strange experiments in eating, once asked me in Rome to dine with him at a very cheap inn outside one of the gates, and he explained how the dinner was arranged. He had found a hostel which did not provide food, but if you bought a lamb from a shepherd outside the gate, so as to save the *octroi*, you could have it cooked in a great pot, a certain amount being charged for the cooking; and you bought your wine, as a matter of course, at the inn. The carters and herds were, he told me, the people who partook of this repast, and every man ate his own lamb, leaving little but the bones. I did not go to that inn. That place of refreshment was at one end of the social ladder, the Grand and Quirinale are at the other. Set a man down in the restaurant of the Grand, or the Winter Garden of the Quirinale, and there will be nothing to give him a hint as to whether he is in London, or Paris, or Rome. He will eat an excellent dinner—French in all respects—and will be waited on by civil waiters, whom he knows to be foreigners, but who will answer him in English whatever language he addresses them in. At either restaurant an excellent dinner of ceremony can be given. The last time that I stayed at the Grand, I ate the *table-d'hôte* dinner on several occasions and found it good. The Roma in the Corso, and the Colonna in the Piazza Colonna, are the typical city restaurants; but they have a leaning towards the French cuisine. To eat the food of Rome, try La Venete in the Via Campo Marzio, which has a garden; or, more distinctive still, the Tre Re, hard by the Pantheon, where you must talk Italian, or else make signs.

Bucci, in the Piazza della Coppelle, is the Scott's or Driver's of Rome, and you can dine or lunch there off shell-fish soup, and the fish which comes from Anzio and the other fishing villages of the coast.

There is a curious restaurant close by the station, Vagliani is, I fancy, the owner, where artichokes are the staple fare, and where the decorations are in keeping with the food. You will find the foreign colony of art students—Danes, Norwegians, Germans—in the restaurants of the Via delle Crace, Coradetti, where the food is well cooked but served without any unnecessary luxury, being perhaps the best eating-house; but the real haunt of the artist in Rome is, at the present time, the Trattoria Fiorella in the Via delle Colonelli. Only do not go and stare at him while he is taking his meals, for if you do, he will go elsewhere to another *trattoria*, the position of which he will keep a dead secret. Of course there are Roman dishes without number, and these are some of the best known of them:—

The *Zuppa di Pesce* is a *Bouillabaisse* without any saffron. The fish and shell-fish (John Dory, red mullet, cuttle-fish, lobster, whiting, muraena, and mussels) which compose it are served on toast. The *Fritto di Calamaretti* is a fry of cuttle-fish in oil. *Cinghiale in agro dolce* is wild boar cooked in a sauce of chocolate, sugar, plums, *pinolis*, red currant, and vinegar. A *bacchio e Capretto alla Cacciatora* is very young lamb and sucking-goat cut into small pieces, and cooked in a sauce to which anchovies and chillies give the dominant taste. *Pollo en padella* are spring chickens cut up and fried with tomatoes, large sweet chillies, and white wine. *Pasticcio di Maccheroni* is an excellent macaroni pie, and *Gnocchi di Patele* are little knobs of paste boiled like macaroni. Broccoli, green peas cooked with butter and ham, and, above all, the Roman artichoke stewed in oil—which is to be obtained at its best in the old Jewish eating-houses of the Ghetto—are the vegetables of Rome. A very small ham is one of the local delicacies. *Gnocchi di latte* are custards in layers, each of which is seasoned with either sugar or butter, or cinnamon or Parmesan cheese; and *Zuppa Inglese* is a rich cake soused with liqueurs and vanilla cream, covered with meringue and baked. *Uova di Bufola* is a little ball of cheese made from buffalo's milk. The best kind, *Abota* is kept in wrappings of fresh myrtle leaves. Marino (red) and Frascati (white) are two of the best local wines. Orvietto has a faint remembrance of the champagne taste. Monte Fiascone is a dessert wine.

Naples

There is a certain man in a certain London club who has a grievance against Italy in general, against Naples in particular, and, to descend to minute detail, against one Neapolitan restaurant above all others. He tells his tale to all comers as a warning to those who *will* travel in "foreign parts." He returned from a long turn of service in India, and, landing at Naples, concluded that as he was in Europe he could get British food. He went to a restaurant which shall be nameless, and ordered a "chump chop." He had the greatest difficulty, through an interpreter, to explain exactly what it was that he wanted, and then was forced to wait for an hour before it appeared. When the bill was presented it frightened him, but the proprietor, on being summoned, said that as such an extraordinary joint had been asked for, he had been compelled to buy a whole sheep to supply it. This is a warning not to ask for British dishes in a Neapolitan restaurant.

Time was when the Gambrinus, which is the excellently decorated café and restaurant at the end of the Chiaja, and the big café and restaurant in the great arcade, were at daggers drawn, and a war of cutting down of prices raged. In those happy days one could dine or lunch at either place sumptuously for a shilling. Some meddling busybody interfered in the quarrel and brought the proprietors into a friendly spirit. The Gambrinus, with its bright rooms, good decorations, and fair attendance, is perhaps the best restaurant at which a stranger can take a meal, unless he is looking for the distinctive Neapolitan cookery. If he is in search of the dishes of the town, let him try the Europa or, better still for his purpose, the Vermouth di Torino in the Piazza del Municipio. To eat the fish dishes which show the real cookery of Naples better than any other, he should go out on a moonlight night a couple of miles to the Antica

Trattoria dello Scoglio di Frisio, or to the less aristocratic Trattoria del Figlio di Pietro in the Strada Nuova del Posilipo.

Of the macaroni I have already written. The splendid tomatoes grown in Naples, which are cooked with it, give it its particular excellence. It is also seasoned with cheese. *Spagetti alle Vongole* is the macaroni seasoned with the little shell-fish of the place. *Zuppa di Vongole* is a clear soup of bread and *Vongole*. *Polpi alla Luciana* are small octopi stewed in an earthern pot with oil, tomatoes, chilli, and red wine. Between the pot and the lid a sheet of oiled paper is placed, to prevent the steam from escaping. The *Spigola*, the most delicate of fishes of the Mediterranean, is at its best between 1 and 1-1/2 lbs. in weight. It is either boiled or roasted, and is served with a sauce of oil, lemon juice, and chopped parsley. A steak *alla Pizzaiola* is baked in an oven with potatoes, garlic, and thyme; and *Pizza alla Pizzaiola* is a kind of Yorkshire pudding eaten either with cheese or anchovies and tomatoes flavoured with thyme. *Mozzarelle in carozza* is a slice of bread soaked in milk and a slice of Provola cheese, the whole plunged in beaten eggs and then fried. There is an excellent Neapolitan method of treating egg-plants, fried in oil, cut in slices, sandwiched with cheese and tomatoes, and then baked. Provola and Cacio Cavallo are the Neapolitan cheeses. Vesuvio, Capri, Gragnano, Lacrima Christa are a few of the wines grown along the bays. The walnuts of Sorrento are the best in Italy.

Palermo

Palermo has its special dishes, amongst them of course its *Spagetti*, seasoned with minced meat and egg-plant; but its ices and its fruit are its particular delicacies. Marsala, Moscato di Siracusa, and Amarena di Siracusa are the wines of the island. If you want to try Sicilian cookery, go either to the Lincoln by the Plazza Marina or the Rebecchina in the Via Vittoria Emanuele.

N.N.-D.

CHAPTER X

SPAIN AND PORTUGAL

Food and wines of the country—Barcelona—San Sebastian—Bilbao—Madrid—Seville—Bobadilla—Grenada—Jerez—Algeciras—Lisbon—Estoril.

A candid Frenchman, who had lived long in Spain, asked as to the cookery of Spain compared with that of other nations, replied, "It is worse even than that of the English, which is the next worst." That Frenchman was, however, rather ungrateful, for the Spaniards taught the French how to stuff turkeys with chestnuts. The Spanish cooks also first understood that an orange salad is the proper accompaniment to a wild duck, and the Spanish hams are excellent. The lower orders in Spain have too great a partiality for *ajo* and *aceite* for oil and garlic. Their oil, which they use greatly even with fish, is not the refined oil of Genoa or the south of France, but is a coarse liquid, the ill taste of which remains all day in one's mouth. Garlic is an excellent seasoning in its proper place and quantity, and the upper classes of the Spaniards have their meat lightly rubbed with it before being cooked, but the lower classes use it in the cooking to an intolerable extent. Capsicum is much eaten in Spain, being sometimes stuffed, but in any quantity it is very indigestible.

In the south of Spain the heat is tropical in the summer, and the only meat then available in any small town is generally goat. As in India, the chicken which you order for your lunch is running about the yard of the inn when the order is given. The principal dish of Spain is *Puchero*, which consists of beef, very savoury sausages, bacon, fowl, and plenty of the white haricot beans known as *garbanzos*, some leeks, and a small onion, all put together into a pot to boil. The liquid is carefully skimmed before it actually boils, and as the scum stops forming hot water is added. The broth, *Caldo*, is used as soup; the remainder, which has had most of the sustaining quality boiled out of it, is the daily dish of the middle and upper classes, who call it *Cocido*. *Gazpaco* is a kind of cold soup much used in the southern and hotter parts of Spain. It is made of bread crumbs, bonito fish, onions, oil, vinegar, garlic, and cucumbers. All these are beaten into a pulp, then diluted, and bread broken into the mixture. The better classes drink this as we should afternoon tea. *Bacalas*, or dried cod, is one of the staple dishes of the poor in the north, and the English in Spain also often eat it. The favourite mode of preparation is to first soak out the salt, then let the cod simmer, but not boil, adding afterwards *pimientas dulces* and chopped onion fried and pounded. The selection of a cod-fish is the first necessity in preparing this dish, for some of the cheaper kinds from Norway are so odoriferous as to make them impossible to most white men.

Spain is a country which is no happy hunting ground for a gourmet. The restaurants in Barcelona one can rely on, Madrid comes next in honour, and the rest, to use a sporting term, are "nowhere," the customary *table-d'hôte* dinner at the restaurants of a small town consisting of *Caldo*, then the universal stew, then *Arroz à la Valencia*, rice, chicken, and tomatoes, and finally quince marmalade.

Lisbon is the one city in Portugal where the cooking is worthy of any serious consideration.

The wines of Spain are the Valdepenàs, which is very strong and really requires eight or ten years in bottle to mature, a Rioja claret, which is a good wine when four years in bottle, and of course sherry in the south, of which all the leading brands are obtainable. In the north I have found Diamante a pleasant wine to drink. The Spanish brandy is, if a good brand is chosen, excellent.

Barcelona

The busy bustling capital of Catalonia is better off in the matter of restaurants than any town in Spain, the capital included. First in order comes Justin's, the longer title of which is the Restaurant de Francia, in the Plaza Real. It is an old-established house with a good cook, and excellent wines in its cellars. It is a restaurant that the French would describe as *non chiffré*, for it does not mark the prices on its card of the day, though they are not higher than at most of the other restaurants of Barcelona. There are some very pleasant private rooms at the restaurant, and a large room for banquets. The cuisine is almost entirely French. You can get a very fair dinner, wine and all, at Justin's for about 6s.; but if you are giving a dinner party, and are prepared to pay 30 pesetas or 18s. a head, Justin's will give you such a dinner as the menu I give below, wine and all:—

Huîtres de Marennes.
Consommé Colbert.
Hors-d'œuvre variés.
Loup. Sauce Hollandaise.
Côtelettes de Sanglier Venaison.
Salmis de Bécasses.
Chapon Truffé.
Petits pois à la crème.
Glace Napolitaine.
Desserts assortis.

Vins.

Rioja blanco.
Vinicola.
Cliquot sec frappé.

The Rioja Blanco, Diamante, and Vinicola seem to be the wines most generally drunk at Justin's. MM. Marius and Gerina are the present proprietors.

In the central square, the Plaza Cataluna, is the new and gorgeous Restaurant Colon, attached to the newly finished hotel of that name. The decorations of the interior are artistic, and the building bears on its façade in gold and colours the arms of the principal European nations. Here, as at Justin's, the cookery is almost entirely of the French school. The *chef* is M. Azcoaga, the manager Mons. Scatti. There is a good fixed priced lunch and dinner, specimen menus of which I give:—

5 Pts. Déjeuner.

Hors-d'œuvre.
Œufs pochés Princesse.
Filets de Sole Waleska.
Poulet Cocotte Bayaldy.
Buffet froid.
Filet grillé. Pommes fondantes.
Biscuit glacé.
Dessert.

6 Pts. Dinner.

Hors-d'œuvre.
Consommé Duchesse.
Crème Windsor.
Turbot. Sauce Hollandaise.

Carré d'Agneau Maintenon.
Haricots verts Anglaise.
Caille sur Canapé.
Salade.
Pêches Richelieu.
Dessert.

The Continental and Martin's may be said to run a dead heat for third place. The former is in the Plaza Cataluna, and its cuisine is both foreign and of the country. On its bill of fare are always three *plats de jour*, and that on one day, *Raviolis Napolitaine*, *Escargots Bourguinonne*, and *Filet grille Bordelaise* were the three dishes, and on another *Œufs Meyerbeer*, *Filet de veau froid aux Légumes*, and *Rap Marinera* shows the variety of the fare. The prices of these dishes are all between one and two pesetas. Under the heading of *fritures*, all kinds of *conchas* and *Escalopitas* and *Croquettas* are to be found, as well as the *Frito Mixto*; and the fish column gives an interesting selection of the sea denizens of the coast, *Rap*, *Calamares*, *Merluza*, *Pouvine*, and others. The banquets at the Continental are entirely French in character.

Martin's in the Rambla del Centro is almost in front of the Opera House, and has a number of snug little rooms for supper parties, of two or more, after the theatre. This is a dinner for a dozen given at Martin's. The position in the menu of game, *hors-d'œuvre*, and fish is in accordance with the usual Spanish custom, and is always adhered to in this establishment:—

VINS.	
Jerez Macharnudo.	Crème de volaille Royale.
	Hors-d'œuvre.
Rioja Clarete.	Cailles à la Maintenon.

Barsac 1893.

Moët Chandon.

Saumon de la Loire à la Parisienne.
Tronçons de Filet à la Périgueux.
Asperges en Branches.
Chapons de la Bresse aux Cressons.
Biscuits Glacés au Praliné.
Dessert assorti.

CAFÉ ET LIQUEURS.

M. Martin, who is the proprietor, will give you a dinner at any price from 4 pesetas upwards. He was caterer to the kings of Portugal and of Sweden when they were at Barcelona in 1888, and has furnished all the banquets given by the municipal council since 1881. *Filet de sole Martin*, one of the dishes of the house, proves that he has the Parisian ambition to give a name to a filleted sole.

The Maison Dorée which has lately been increased to double its original size, has as proprietors the MM. Pompidor, Frenchmen, who march with the times. It is in the Plaza Cataluna. It makes a speciality of a *prix-fixe* breakfast and dinner on Thursdays and Saturdays, and it serves tea daily *à l'Anglaise* from 4 to 6.

PORT BOU

There is a little restaurant at Port Bou, kept by Francisco Jaque, where you are likely, if you are making a stay to see the Pyrenees, to be better looked after than at the station on the French side of the frontier. There are rooms to be hired there.

SAN SEBASTIAN

Crossing the Spanish frontier on the western side from France, the first important town reached is San Sebastian. The great sea-bathing place of Spain is a town where one would expect to find some excellent restaurants, for the Queen-mother lives for a great part of the year in her palace on the sea-shore, and the Court is with the King whenever he is in residence there, which is generally in summer and autumn. A large hotel, with a good restaurant and all the latest improvements, is projected, and no doubt San Sebastian will soon be as well catered for as any French watering-place; but in the meantime it is as well for the casual seeker for a meal to go to the Continental, which overlooks the bay, and where a very fair breakfast is to be obtained for 4 francs in the verandah whence all the life of the place can be watched.

The Casino has a restaurant with a wide verandah which should be a delightful place at which to take dinner. I had been warned that I should not be well served there, but one day I thought that the view of the town and the garden, with its picturesque crowd, would make amends for any dilatoriness. This was the menu of the dinner that I partook of, and, though wine was included in the repast, to conciliate the haughty Spaniard in dress-clothes who came and looked at me as though I were an "earth-man," I ordered a pint of Diamante:—

Hors-d'œuvre.

POTAGES.

Crème de volaille. Consommé Riche.

POISSON.

Langouste. Sauce Tartare.

ENTRÉE.

Salmis de Perdreaux au Jerez.

Légumes.

Tomates farcies Provençale.

Rôti.

Filet de Bœuf Piqué Broche. Salade.

Entremets.

Arlequin. Dessert.

I do not think that I ever had a worse-served 7 francs worth of food. Once in my life, at a Chicago hotel, I saw a negro waiter shaking up the bottle of Burgundy I had ordered, just to amuse his brother "coons," and I felt a helpless exasperation as I watched him. The same feeling of voiceless anger was upon me as I watched the gentleman who was supposed at the San Sebastian Casino to keep me supplied with hot food, bring a dish from the interior of the café and then put it down on somebody else's table to cool while he strolled across the terrace to ask the military guardian at the gate how many people had paid for admission, or at what hour the band played, or what number had won the lottery.

Bourdette and the Urbana, both with French cookery, are the restaurants patronised by the Englishmen in San Sebastian who talk Spanish, and both are said to be fairly good.

Bilbao

It is curious that at the great northern town of Spain there should be no first-class restaurants. The two best in the town are the Antiguo, in the Calle de Bidebarrieta, and the Moderno. Both of these boast what the Spaniards term *Cocina Francesa*, which only means that if you make a request, as the English always do, the cook will fry your food with butter instead of oil.

At Portugalete, the port of Bilbao, there is a restaurant, good, as Spanish restaurants go, attached to the hotel of the place, the proprietor of which is Dn. Manuel Calvo. The cook and the staff of waiters come from Lhardy's, the best restaurant in Madrid, and spend their summer by the seaside. The prices at this restaurant are high. Portugalete is only a summer resort.

Northern Towns

At Santander, a little further along the northern coast, the best food to be obtained is found at the Hôtel Europa; but the best is bad at Santander. At Burgos and at Zaragoza the two largest hotels in each place give the least indifferent food.

Madrid

The capital of Spain cries aloud for a Carlton, or a Ritz, or a Savoy, and is, I believe, soon to have a really large hotel with a restaurant managed on the lines which we are accustomed to in all the important European capitals. The Hôtel de Paris, one of the two noisy and expensive hotels on the Puerta del Sol, has always had a reputation for its cookery, always remembering that the standard in Spain is not high. There is a *table-d'hôte* lunch and a *table-d'hôte* dinner, of the latter of which I append a menu which is a fair specimen:—

Consommé Julienne.
Merlan Sauce aux Câpres.
Filet de Bœuf Renaissance.
Galantine Truffée à l'Aspic.

Haricots Verts Sautés.
Cailles au Cresson.
Crème au Chocolat Glacée.
Desserts assortis.

The cookery of the house is French, but Spanish dishes can be obtained by an order given in advance. There used to be a manager at the Paris who was known as Constantino—what his other name was no one knew. He was a universal provider, and the Englishmen who knew him and who used to stay at the Madrid, never hesitated to ask him for anything procurable in the capital, from a ticket for a bull-fight to a genuine Murillo, quite sure that next morning they would find in the office what they had asked for the previous evening.

Lhardy's, in the Curera de San Jerónimo, is the typical Madrid restaurant not attached to an hotel. The appearance of the ground floor is that of a *charcutier's* and pastry-cook's combined. The restaurant you will find on the first floor, where a *table-d'hôte* dinner and lunch are served. The annexed menu shows what the daily lunch is like:—

Potage Tortue à l'Américaine.
Turbot Garni. Sauce Crevettes.
Filets de Bœuf à la Vatel.
Bellevue de Perdreaux à l'Ecarlate.
Dindonneaux rôtis au Cresson.
Salade Russe.
Glace Condé.
Dessert.

VINS.

Jeréz.
Bordeaux.

Champagne Frappé.
Café and Liqueurs.

The Café de Fornos is also well spoken of by all who have experimented. The restaurant at the Fornos is in the café on the ground floor. On the first floor are the private rooms. There are several of the restaurants with *cabinets particuliers* where little suppers are given after the theatre, the Fornos being one; but the Madrilese dandy, wishing to sup *à deux*, generally chooses the Café Inglés, as the private rooms are very well decorated. The Perla is also well spoken of. All these restaurants profess the French cuisine, and at Lhardy's as good a dinner is obtainable as at the best restaurants of Barcelona.

Seville

At Seville you dine and breakfast at your hotel, whether it be the Madrid or the Paris, both very good hotels for Spain. There is a *table-d'hôte* dinner at each after the style of the meal of which I have given a menu under the heading of Madrid. At both hotels an extra charge is made to those aristocrats who will not sit at the long table which runs down the centre of the highly ornamented dining-room and are accommodated at little tables at the sides of the room. The great *patio* of the Madrid, with its palm grove and creepers, is a delightful place to sit in after dinner.

The dinner-hour at Seville is seven o'clock. There is a Restaurant Suizo in the Calle de las Sierpes, and a little restaurant, the Eritana, with a pleasant garden, is to be found near the turning point of the drive that the beauty and fashion of Seville take on fine afternoons down the Paseo de las Delicias by the river. If you are tempted to try the Manzanilla wine with its proper accompaniment of snails or *langostinos*, visit the Taberna, opposite the Madrid Hotel; and if you are a bachelor, do not mind an atmosphere of smoke, can make yourself understood in Spanish, and like local colour, take your *café au lait* of an evening in the Café Cantante of the Calle Sterpes. You will recognise the house by the little dancing-girl on the lamp.

Bobadilla

The junction of the lines to Seville, Granada, and Algeciras is Bobadilla, and there all trains wait for half an hour that the passengers may feed. The meal is a very fair sample of Spanish cookery, and you are given soup or eggs, according to the time of day, an entrée, a joint, and fish. I can still recall a Bobadillian meal, with the taste of garlic acting as a sort of *Leitmotiv* in all the dishes, of omelette, stewed beef and beans, a ragout of veal, fried fish in butter, and cheese. Do not omit to cast an eye on the fair damsel behind the bar. She is a typical Andalusian beauty and is used to admiration.

Grenada

The hotels Siete Suclos and Washington Irving are the two principal hotels near the Alhambra, and are crowded with tourist-trippers of all nations, Americans and Germans predominating, during the tourist season. At the Siete Suclos the cookery is said to be Spanish in character. My personal experience is confined to the Washington Irving, and on the first day of my stay, when I tried to order breakfast and the waiter, in answer to my query as to what dishes were ready, rolled out with great rapidity, "Beefsteeake, colfolanam, baconnegs, mutton-chops, mutton cotolettes," I thought that the local Spanish dishes sounded something like English ones. Englishmen who live in Spain tell me that they generally go to the Alhambra, which I take to be the Casa de Huespedes, 3 Alhambra, a lodging-house where I fancy only Spanish is spoken.

Cadiz and Jerez

At Cadiz the cooking at the Grand Hôtel de Paris is Spanish and good of its kind. At Jerez the cooking at the Fondas de Los Cisnes and La Victoria is Spanish also. This is the menu of a dinner at the Hôtel Los Cisnos:—

>Consommé de Quenelles á la Royal.
>Filetes de Tenguados á la Tutus.
>Chuletas de Cordero á la Inglesa.
>Pechugas de Pollos á la Suprema.
>Perdices al jugo.
>Ensalada Rusa.
>Espárragos de Aranjuez, salsa blanca.
>Mantecados de Vainilla y Fresa.
>Postres variados.

Algeciras

The town on the Spanish side of the bay has redeemed Gibraltar from its ill fame as a place of entertainment. The late Ignacio Lersundi, under whose rule the Bristol in London—now converted into a ladies' club—gave one of the best, if not the best, *table-d'hôte* dinners obtainable in the English capital, supervised the arrangements of the Hôtel Reina Christina, and the *table-d'hôte* dinner there still is an excellent one.

Lisbon

There are good hotels to stay at in Lisbon and there are restaurants in plenty, but to try the cookery of some of the town eating-houses a gourmet requires to have his taste educated up to, or down to, the Portuguese standard.

At the Braganza, a little club of bachelor Britons have been in the habit of dining together and ordering their dinner in advance, and this is a fair sample of what the steady-going but very comfortable hostelry can do when it chooses:—

	POTAGES.
Madeira Riche.	Queues de Bœuf. Crème Clamart.
	Petits Soufflés Desir.
Johannisberger (Claus).	Saumon Sauce Genèvoise.
	Selle de Présalé à la Montpensier.
	Poularde à l'Ambassadrice.
Château Giscours.	Pain de foies gras en Bellevue.
	Punch au Kirsch.
	Asperges Sauce Mousseuse.
George Goulet, 1892 Vintage.	Pintades Truffées.
	Salade Japonaise.
	Timbales à la Lyon d'Or.
Porto 1815.	Glaces à la Américaine.
	Petits fours.
	Dessert.
Liqueurs.	Café.

A good *table-d'hôte* breakfast and dinner are served daily at 11 A.M. and 7 P.M. and the price is moderate, being about 800 réis and 1.200 respectively. (It is well to remember that the exchange varies considerably, and it is therefore difficult to give the equivalents in sterling for the prices quoted, but 5500 to 6000 réis may be roughly taken at £1 sterling.) The proprietor is M. Sasetti, who is ably supported by his manager and by a head waiter named Celestino, a most useful person in every way.

Wines, spirits, and liqueurs of foreign origin are expensive at the Braganza, as they are everywhere else, owing to the high custom tariff; but the local wines, amongst which may be cited Collares, Cadafaes,

Collares Branco, Serradayres white and red, etc., are all good and cheap table wines.

The next restaurant as regards comfort, cleanliness, and cuisine is the Café Tavares, situated in the Rua Largo de S. Roque. It is essentially a café restaurant, and is open from breakfast time in the morning till 3 or 4 the following morning. Tavares is the principal rendezvous of the young bloods, both Portuguese and foreign, particularly so after the theatres and opera are over and suppers are in demand. The revel goes on from twelve o'clock until any hour of the morning, more especially as regards the *cabinets particuliers*, which are best entered from the back entrance situated in the Rua das Gaveas. A very good *table-d'hôte* lunch and dinner are served daily at the very moderate cost of 600 and 800 reis. The proprietor and manager is Snr. Caldeira, who is most attentive and obliging to his guests.

If any visitor to Lisbon is anxious to try the Portuguese cooking, he cannot do better than pay a visit to the Leão d'Ouro, situated in the Rua de Principe, adjoining the Central Railway Station. This formerly was, and to a great extent still is, the rendezvous of actors, authors, and professional men. The food is good and very cheap, served *à la carte*. Portuguese food may be called "highly seasoned," but for all that there are many good dishes, one speciality of the house being *Sopa de Camarao*, a *bisque* of prawns, which in no way is to be despised. With regard to wines at this restaurant it is advisable to drink those of the country.

Estoril

Estoril is a very picturesque and beautiful spot about three-quarters of an hour from Lisbon by rail. Here there has been lately established a high-class hotel with *cuisine à la Française* and good wines. The hotel is owned and managed by M. Estrade, who has had a long experience in this class of business.

N.N.-D.

CHAPTER XI

AUSTRIA AND HUNGARY

Viennese restaurants and cafés—Baden—Carlsbad—Marienbad—Prague—Bad Gastein—Budapesth.

Vienna

The cuisine of the best of the Viennese restaurants, those attached to the big hotels, is French, though the Wiener Rostbraten and the Wiener Schnitzel are world-famous, and the typical Viennese dinner is a good French dinner with the addition of very delicious bread and pastry made with a lighter hand than any Gallic cook brings to his task. The wines of the country of Retz, Mailberg, Pfaffstadt, Gumpoldskirchen, Klosterneuberg, Nussberg, and Vöslau should all be tasted, most of them being more than drinkable. Beer, however, is the real Viennese drink, and the very light liquid, ice cold, is a delightful beverage.

"Stay at what hotel you please, but dine at the Bristol," was the advice given me nigh a score of years ago when I first visited Vienna, and it holds good now; indeed of late the "smart set" of Vienna has taken it greatly into favour, and dines or sups there—the opera and plays begin at 7 and end at 10—constantly. The prices, *à la carte*, are high, but the cooking is good. Some specialities of the house are trout taken alive from the aquarium, *Huitres Titania, Homard Cardinal, Poularde Wladimir, Soufflé King Edward VII., Oranges à l'Infante.*

Sacher's, in the hotel of that name just behind the Opera House, is very well known and may be taken as the typical Viennese restaurant. It is expensive, as indeed all the best Viennese restaurants are. It is not quite so exclusively French in its cuisine as some of the other good restaurants, and one of its *plats de jour* is always a national dish, as often as not a Hungarian one, so that by dining or breakfasting at Sacher's one obtains some idea of what the real cookery of the dual monarchy is like. Sacher's has a branch establishment in the Prater, which is always in high favour with the Viennese.

Hartmann's (Leidinger's successor) in the Ring, is an excellent restaurant to breakfast at. Here more of the national dishes—the pickled veal, smoked sucking pig, stewed beef of various kinds, Risi-Bisi, stewed pork—are to be found than at the restaurants mentioned above. It is rather Bohemian, but only pleasantly so.

A good word may be said for the cooking at Meissl and Schadn's, in the Kärnthenerstrass, and for that at the Reidhof.

The Stephan Keller (Café de l'Europe) in the Stephan Platz is a much frequented café. It was originally an underground resort in the vaults of St-Stephan, but it has risen to a higher sphere. This house is much used by the colony of artists who also are to be found at Hartmann's, Gause's, and the Rother Igel.

There are wine houses—Esterhazy Keller, for instance, where all classes go to drink the Hungarian wines from the estates of Prince Esterhazy—without number, and many of these have their speciality of Itrian or Dalmatian wines. The summer resorts are mostly for the people only; they are butterfly cafés opening in the summer and closing in the winter, and if their *clientèle* deserts them there are only some painted boards, tables, and benches to be carted away and a hedge to be dug out; but in the Prater there are some more substantial establishments, Sacher's, mentioned before, and the Rondeau and Lusthaus, which are made the turning-points in the daily drives of the Viennese.

Vienna keeps very early hours, the cafés closing well before midnight, unless they are kept open for some special *fête*.

In the environs of Vienna there are pleasant restaurants on the Kalenberg, up which a little railway runs, and at Klosterneuberg, where one can drink the excellent wine of the place at the Stiftskeller before one admires the view from the terrace or looks at the treasures of the abbey.

Baden

Baden bei Wien is a little watering-place sixteen miles from the capital, to which the Viennese go for a "cure," and to which the Carlsbad and Marienbad doctors sometimes send their patients to begin an after cure. It is a pretty little place with shady parks and an unpretentious restaurant at the Kurhaus and another in the Weilburggasse, and the walk up the valley of the Schwechat has café-restaurants at several of the points of interest.

Carlsbad

Probably twenty Englishmen go to Carlsbad for their liver's sake for every ten who go to Vienna to be amused, and the great Bohemian town in the valley where the hot spring gushes up is one of the resorts to which gourmets, who have eaten not wisely but too well, are most frequently sent. It is a town of good but very simple fare, for the doctors rule it absolutely, and nothing which can hurt a patient's digestion is allowed to appear on the bill of fare of any of the restaurants or hotels.

The life of the place, which chiefly is bound up in the consideration of where to eat the three simple meals allowed, is curious. In the morning, after the disagreeable necessity of drinking three or more glassfuls of the hot water, every man and every lady spends a half hour deciding where to breakfast and what kind of roll and what kind of ham they shall eat. The bakers' shops are crowded by people picking out the special rusk or special roll they prefer, and these are carried off in little pink bags. Two slices of ham are next bought from one of the shops where men in white clothes slice all day long at the lean Prague ham or the fatter Westphalian. No man is really a judge of ham until he has argued for a quarter of an hour every morning outside the shop in the Carlsbad High Street as to what breed of pig gives the most appetising slice. Bag in hand, ham in pocket, the man undergoing a cure walks to the Elephant in the Alte Wiese, or to one of the little restaurants which stud the valley and the hillsides, delightful little buildings with great glass shelters for rainy days and lawns and flower-beds and creepers, where neat waitresses in black, with their Christian names in white metal worn as a brooch, or great numbers pinned to their shoulders, receive you with laughing welcome, set a red-clothed table for you, and bring you the hot milk and boiled eggs which complete your repast. Be careful of which waitress you smile at on your first day, for she claims you as her especial property for the rest of your stay, and to ask another waitress to bring your eggs would be the deepest treason.

Dinner is a mid-day meal, and as you are not tied down to any particular hotel for your meals because you happen to be staying in it, the custom is to dine where your fancy pleases you. There is Pupp's with its verandah and its little grove of Noah's ark trees, patronised by all nations, and the Golden Shield and Anger's, and Wirchaupt's in the Alte Wiese, which since I have known Carlsbad has grown from a ham shop into a very smart little restaurant handsomely decorated. Wirchaupt's is small enough still for its patrons to have individual attention paid them, and if you are an *habitué* you will be told as you go in if anything especially good has been bought at market that morning, and little hints are given you as to the composition of your meal. Bohemian partridges and the trout and *Zander* from the Tepl and other mountain streams are the two great "stand-bys" of the man at Carlsbad who likes good food; but the big fowls which come, I fancy, from Styria, are excellent birds; the venison, the hares, the mutton, and the ever-present ham are all capital. The wines of the country are excellent. The cheapest form of the local wine is served in little *caraffes*, but here, as in most other places, it is wise to pay the extra shilling and drink the bottled wine. Besides the wine of the province there are obtainable the usual Austrian wines, and the Hungarian Erlauer and Offner and Carlowitz.

I have halted in the Alte Wiese to descant on the usual dinner of Carlsbad, which, ordered *à la carte*, never costs more than a few shillings. Up on the hill at the Bristol, from the terrace of which there is a fine view over the valley to the Keilberg, and at the Savoy Westend, where some Egyptian servants imported by Nuncovitch from the land of the Pharoahs wait upon you, and which has a great pavilion as its open-air dining-hall, you are likely to find most of the people, English and American, whose movements are recorded in the society papers, taking their mid-day meal. The American millionaire at Carlsbad, however, fares just as simply and just as cheaply as does any half-pay captain, for Dr. Krauss and Dr. London are no considerers of persons in their dieting.

In the afternoon, about five o'clock, all the world goes to one of the cafés in the valley to listen to a concert and to drink hot milk; and in the evening a meal, as simple as dinner has been, is eaten. This is the hour to see Pupp's at its best. In the little grove of trees before the house, where the big band-stand is, there is an array of tables, each with its lamp upon it. In the outside verandah of the great restaurant there are more tables, and inside the glazed verandah and in two long rooms, each rising a step above the other, are a host of people supping. The scene is like some great effect at a theatre, and I know nowhere where one can find any restaurant shining with light as Pupp's does on a summer night. The restaurant in the Stadtpark is always crowded when the band plays there, but the attendance is very hurried and casual, and contrasts badly with Pupp's and the other first-class restaurants. At the two Variety Theatres in the lower town one can, by booking a table in advance, sup fairly comfortably, and listen while one sups to a very good variety entertainment.

At Gieshübl, where Herr Mattoni makes a fortune by bottling the spring water, and which is little more than an hour's drive from Carlsbad, there is an excellent restaurant where the fare is the same as that found in Carlsbad.

Marienbad

All that I have written of Carlsbad, concerning its food and drink, applies to Marienbad. There is the same freedom as to dining-places, and on a sunny day a man will take his meal in one of the creeper-grown bowers which are erected on the edge of the park by the hotels which face it, or at the Kursaal garden. On a dull day he will dine at Klinger's, the house which has a special celebrity, but which, with its rather stuffy rooms and its much ornamented plate-glass windows, which never seem to open quite wide enough, is pleasanter on a cool day than a hot one; or at the New York, which has its rooms ornamented after the style the Parisians call "the New Art."

There are several good restaurants in the environs of Marienbad, at the Waldmühle and elsewhere, and the Egerländer Café is well worth a visit. It is a large café, with the usual grove before it, built on a commanding hill. The special characteristics of the place are that the rooms and the great hall are built and furnished after the fashion of Egerland, the most picturesque style that Austria boasts of. The girls who wait are all in the handsome Egerland costume, and the effect is very pretty. There is a restaurant at Egerland, and the proprietor, when I was at Marienbad in 1901, talked of adding sleeping apartments to the establishment and of making it a hotel as well as a restaurant and café.

Prague

The expedition to Prague generally forms part of a stay at Carlsbad or Marienbad. My personal experience, gained from two visits, is that if one stays either at the Saxe or the Blauer Stern, it is wiser to take one's meals in the restaurants of the hotels than to go further afield and fare worse. One traverses the hop-fields of Pilsen during the journey from Carlsbad, and an amateur of beer should find Prague a paradise second only to Munich.

Bad Gastein

There are several more or less pretentious hotels in Gastein, but perhaps the most reliable for feeding purposes is the Badeschloss; it is rather old-fashioned, but good of its kind. It was formerly the palace of the Cardinal Bishops. The hot-water springs, discovered in A.D. 680, have their source close to the hotel.

Budapesth

The most distinctive feature of Hungarian cookery is the use of *paprika*, the national pepper. A *Goulache*, as it is usually written on menus, or *Gulyas* as the Hungarians call it, is a ragout in which the pepper plays an important part. The *Paprikahuhn* is a chicken stewed or baked with the pepper, which is very pleasant tasting. Pork served with a sharp-tasting *purée* in which cranberries play a *rolé*, and other combinations of meat and fruit, brought together very much as we Britons take red current jelly with hare and mutton, are all part of the national cookery. The entrails of animals are used to make some of the dishes; pork, from the innocent sucking pig to the great wild boar, veal, pickled or fresh, and calves lungs in vinegar are all treated as national dishes.

The wines of the country are well known to all Anglo-Saxons for some of them, the red wines, Erlauer, Ofner, and Carlovicz, are exported in great quantities. The white wines, Ruster, Schomlayer, Szegszarder, and others are equally drinkable, while Tokay is of course a king amongst wines.

Of restaurants in Budapesth there are but few to be recommended to the wanderer. Both the Ungaria and the Koningen von England have restaurants where one can order a dinner which is expensive however simple it may be, and where one may listen to one of those gipsy bands which are now to be found in most of the London restaurants and in some of the Parisian ones. The best restaurant not attached to an hotel is Palkowitch's, the National Casino, which is the "smart" restaurant of the town. A Hungarian gentleman, wishing to give a friend a good dinner, takes him to the Casino Club, and this is the style of meal and wines that he will get. I am not responsible for the spelling of the menu, which is that of the club steward:—

Somtoi.	Gulzas Clair.
Eteville 1868.	Fogas de Balaton à la Jean Bart.
Château Margaux 1875.	Cuissot de Porc frais.
	Choucroute farcie.
Moet 1884.	Cailles rôties sur Canapé Salade.
Tokay 1846.	Artichauts frais. Sauce Bordelaise.
Silvorium 1796.	Turos Lepeny.
Baracrkpalinka 1860.	

There is a fairly good restaurant near the landing-place on the Margarethen Insel.

N.N.-D.

CHAPTER XII

ROUMANIA

The dishes of the country—The restaurants of Bucarest.

In Roumania you must never be astonished at the items set down in the bill of fare, and if "bear" happens to be one try it, for bruin does not make at all bad eating. The list of game is generally surprisingly large, and one learns in Roumania the difference there is in the venison which comes from the different breeds of deer. Caviar, being the produce of the country, is a splendid dish, and you are always asked which of the three varieties, easily distinguishable by their variety of colour, you will take. A caviar *salade* is a dish very frequently served. The following are some of the dishes of the country:—*Ciulama*, chicken with a sauce in which flour and butter are used; *Scordolea*, in which crawfish, garlic, minced nuts, and oil all play a part; *Baclava*, a cake of almonds served with *sirop* of roses. These three dishes, though now Roumanian, were originally introduced from Turkey. *Ardei Ungelute* is a dish of green pepper, meat, and rice; *Sarmalute* are vine leaves filled with meat and served with a preparation of milk; *Militei* is minced beef fried on a grill in the shape of a sausage. *Cheslas* and *Mamaliguzza*, the food of the peasant, much resemble the Italian *Polenta* and are eaten with cold milk. *Ghiveci*, a ragout with all kinds of vegetables mixed in it, is a great dish of the country.

Bucarest

When in Bucarest, as it should be spelt, go straight to Capsa's in the Calea Victorici, a first-rate restaurant. It is perhaps not quite equal to the best of the London and Paris establishments, but the cooking is really good, and certainly superior to anything you can find in Vienna. The French *chef* will provide you with a *récherché* dinner ordered *à la carte*. Fresh caviar is in perfection there, as also the sterlet or young sturgeon; the latter is caught in the Danube, and is a most dainty and much prized fish. The prices are fairly high,—about 2 francs 50 centimes for an ordinary *plat*. The wines are all rather expensive, that of the country being perhaps best left alone, although the Dragasani is a wine which tastes strangely at first, but to which one becomes used. A liqueur tasting of carraway seeds is pleasant, but that made from the wild plum is not to be rashly ventured upon.

This is the menu of a little dinner for two eaten at Capsa's:—

>Caviar.
>Ciorba de Poulet.
>Turbot à la Grec.
>Mousaka aux Courzes.
>Gâteaux.

And this a breakfast at the same establishment:—

>Glachi de Carpe (froid).
>Œufs Polenta.
>Pilau.
>Aubergines aux Tomates.

There is also a confectioner's shop kept by Capsa, who was for some considerable time at Boissier's in Paris, afterwards returning to Bucarest and opening this establishment. It is as good as that of any Parisian *confiseur*, with the result that all Bucarest are his customers, and his business is an extremely lucrative one.

A cheap dinner can be obtained, *à la carte*, at the Hôtel Continental in the Calea Victorici, opposite the Théâtre Nationale.

Jordachi's in the Strada Coatch, and Enesco's in the Strada Sfantu Tonica, also deserve mention; they are cheap, second-rate restaurants, but you get there the dishes of the country. In both these places a capital band of Tziganes play the music of the country. Enesco's is, perhaps, the better of the two. If you require any *spécialités* the waiter will be sure to know what to advise; one dish, called *Brochettes de Filet*, may be recommended. The waiters at Enesco's and Jordachi's are intelligible in German and Roumanian; at the Continental, and especially at Capsa's, they are mostly French.

If you pay a call in Bucarest you will be offered *Dolceazza*, a kind of sweetmeat, and a glass of water.

CHAPTER XIII

SWEDEN. NORWAY. DENMARK

Stockholm restaurants—Malmö—Storvik—Gothenburg—Christiana—Copenhagen—Elsinore.

STOCKHOLM

Of all the restaurants in the capital of Sweden the Hasselbacken, in the Royal Djurgarten Park, is the most interesting to visit should it be open, which it is from the beginning of March till the end of September. During the early part of the season Tziganes play in one of the small rooms, whereas in summer a somewhat noisy orchestra plays in the garden. The price of dinner, *à prix fixe*, is 3 kronor 50 öre; this includes soup, fish, meat, *relevé* (generally a Swedish guinea-fowl called *hjärpe*) and ice. Wine and coffee are of course extra.

The Hasselbacken is often used for the giving of banquets of ceremony, but the dinner at 3 kr. 50 öre is more likely to interest the stranger within the gates than the more extensive feasts, so I give a typical menu of this very reasonably priced repast:—

Purée à la Reine.
Saumon fumé aux Epinards.
Selle de Mouton aux Légumes.
Gelinottes rôties. Salade.
Soufflée au Citron.

Quite one of the best restaurants is in the Hôtel Continental opposite the Railway Station. The food here is excellent, *tornedos* (1 kr. 50 öre) and *nässelkalsoppa*, an excellent soup made from a sort of young nettle, being specialities. The prices are slightly cheaper than those of the Hasselbacken.

Operakällaren is a very good restaurant and one of the most popular. They serve here a *déjeuner* at 1 kr. 50 öre consisting of an excellent dish of eggs (a speciality of the place) and meat and cheese or so-called "sweet" (generally a very unwholesome stale cake with cream). The *table-d'hôte* dinners are excellent, one being at 3 kr. 50 öre and the other at 2 kr. 50 öre; the first consisting of soup (thick soups being a speciality of the place), fish, entrée, meat, and *relevé* (generally *hjärpe*), with a *compote* of Swedish berries called lingon (a sort of cranberry) and an indifferent sweet or ice. Here, as in most Swedish eating-places, objection is taken to coffee being served in the restaurants, people being requested to take it in the café, which is generally the next room. Supper is served at the Operakällaren, and the restaurant is crowded for this meal. It costs 2 kronor and consists of a *smörgasbord* or copious *hors-d'œuvre*, an entrée, and meat.

The Grand Hotel is fairly popular, owing to the smartness of the dining-room and the "swagger" way in which meals are served. The food is not as good as the decorations. The lunch costs 2 kr. 50 öre and the dinner 3 kr. 50 öre.

The Hôtel Rydberg is also most popular, and the food is good. A great feature is made here, as everywhere, of the *smörgasbord* (literally "bread and butter") table, which has a room to itself and on which are a score or more of dishes, there being some wonderful combinations of smoked eels and other fish and eggs amongst them. There are from five to thirty of these dishes, all delicate and appetising. The guests eat them standing. In the same room is a huge plated spirit-stand containing a number of different spirits, white brandy called "Branvin," and other drinks resembling Vodka. The crayfish, *kråftor*, a little larger than the

French ones, excellent in flavour and served in a terrine, the *bisque* soup, *caviar* served, as of course it should be, on a bed of ice are good at the Rydberg and the cook manages to make even a ptarmigan toothsome. It is a favourite place for people to sup at after the theatre. The *table-d'hôte* dinner costs 3 kr. 50 öre and the lunch 2 kr. 50 öre. Caloric punch is a favourite drink here, as elsewhere in Sweden, and two men think nothing of drinking a bottle between them after dinner or supper.

The Café du Nord is very crowded and very popular, although more bourgeois than the others. The food is good, meals being served mostly *à la carte*. A good *filet de bœuf* costs about 90 öre. The business men who mostly patronise this café dine from 3 to 4 P.M. Many people sup there in the evening. There are some excellently painted pictures in black and gold, rather daring and French in subject, on the walls.

There are also the Café Anglais (fairly good) and the Hamburger Börs. The Berns' Salonger, the Blanch Café and Strömparterren are cafés where coffee, punch, liqueurs, and sandwiches may be had. The former is the only one open in summer and winter, the two latter being opened on 1st May without regard to the temperature, and closed on 30th September.

Malmö

At Malmö, which is the landing place from Kiel, there is a good dinner or lunch obtainable at the big hotel with twin turrets which faces the statue to Gustavus Adolphus.

Storvik

At Storvik, a station on the Storlieu line, there is a restaurant which is celebrated throughout Sweden. You are charged 2 kronor, which is the price of a meal at all railway refreshment rooms, and help yourself at a big central table, crayfish soup, fish, meat, poultry, game, and sweets all being included in the meal, and a glass of light beer.

GOTHENBURG

The restaurant of the Haglund is a good one, and I give one of the menus of its dinner at 3 kronor:—

SOPPA.

Potage à la Parmentier.

FISK.

Saumon grillée à la maître d'hôtel.

KÖTTRÄTT.

Langue de Bœuf Garni. Sauce aux Olives, ou Fricandeau de veau aux pois.

STEK.

Poulet à la Printanier. Compotes.

EFTERRÄTT.

Bavaroise hollandaise ou Framboises.

National Dishes

There are very few Swedish national dishes, milk, cream, butter, and fish being, however, excellent. The *Smörgasbord* is the great institution of the country. *Plättar*, or Swedish pancakes, are also good.

Norway

Norway is by no means a happy hunting ground for the gourmet. Salmon, halibut, and ptarmigan are the usual luxuries, and they pall on the palate after a time. The Hôtel Victoria at Christiana is well spoken of in the matter of cooking, and the Brittania at Throndhjem is said to cater well considering the latitude it is situated in.

Denmark

From the gourmet's point of view there is little to write as to the Copenhagen restaurants. That of the Hôtel d'Angleterre is good, and a good word can also be said for the cooking at the Hôtel Phœnix.

The Tivoli Gardens are the summer resort of Copenhagen, and all classes patronise them, rich and poor both being catered for. They are a magnified Earl's Court, with the Queen's Hall and the booths from a French fair added. There are restaurants of all kinds at the Tivoli, some being very popular and surprisingly cheap. One of these restaurants, the Danish one, is of interest and gives a very good national meal for 3 kronor.

The Café National is an excellent place at which to sup, cold poached eggs in aspic being one of the delicacies of the house.

All the world makes expeditions to Elsinore, or as the Danes, regardless of Shakespeare, call it, Helingsör. There in the Marienlyst you may see Hamlet's grave, which is so excellently built up that one would believe it to be really the burial place of a Viking, and you can lunch at the Kursaal, whence there is a delightful view across the Sound to Sweden. There is a second park at Elsinore where Ophelia's pool is shown.

The meals in Denmark are preceded by a feast of little delicacies, "sandwiches with the roof off" as they have been aptly described, which both men and ladies eat as they stand and chat before going into lunch or dinner, as is the custom in Sweden and Russia also.

N.N.-D.

CHAPTER XIV

RUSSIA

Food of the country—Restaurants in Moscow—The dining places of St. Petersburg—Odessa—Warsaw.

Russian Dishes

The Russians are a nation of gourmands, for the *Zakouska*, the potatoes and celery, spiced eels, stuffed crayfish, chillies stuffed with potato, olives, minced red cabbage, smoked goose-flesh, smoked salmon, smoked sturgeon, raw herring, pickled mushrooms, radishes, caviar, and a score of other "appetisers," and the *petits patés*, the *Rastegai* (tiny pies of the lightest paste with a complicated fish stuffing and a little fresh caviar in the openings at the top), the *Tartelettes St-Hubert*, any other little pasties of fish and flesh eaten with the soup, could only be consumed by vigorous eaters. Soups are the contribution of Russia to the cuisine of the world, and the moujik, when he first stirred some sour cream into his cabbage broth, little thought that from his raw idea the majestic *Bortch* would come into existence. The two cold soups of which salt cucumber juice forms the foundation are curious. There are other admirable soups of Russian invention, one, *Selianka*, a fish soup made from the sterlet and sturgeon, being much liked when a taste for it has been acquired. The sturgeon of course comes into the menu of many Russian dinners, and also the sterlet, cooked in white wine and served with shrimp sauce.

There is a fish pie of successive layers of rice, eggs, and fish, which is one of the native dishes and is much like *Kedgeree*. Boiled Moscow sucking pig, which in its short but happy life has tasted naught but cream, boiled and served with horse-radish sauce and sour cream is a dish for good angels, and roast mutton stuffed with buckwheat is not to be despised. *Srazis* are little rolled strips of mutton with forced meat inside, fried in butter. Moscow is especially celebrated for its cutlets of all kinds, chicken garnished with mushrooms and cream, and veal in especial. *Nesselrode Pudding* is frequently found on Russian menus. Some of the peasant soups, one for instance in which all the scraps of the kitchen are boiled with any grain and fruit which may be handy, are dreadful decoctions. Russia has its native wines, those of the Caucasus being very good imitations of French wine. There is a champagne of the Don which often finds its way into bottles with French labels on them. Polynnaïa, a wormwood whisky, is an excellent digestive.

I now let A.B. have his say.

Moscow

There are three principal restaurants in Moscow—the Bolskoi Moscovski, the Ermitage, and the Slaviansky Bazaar; of these the Ermitage and the Bolskoi are probably the best for dinner.

The Ermitage in Trubnaia Plastchad has a great reputation in Moscow for its cuisine, and is the favourite restaurant and resort of the upper class; it has an imposing general luncheon and dining-hall, also separate saloons for private dinner-parties. Most of the official banquets are held here.

The cost of a luncheon, with choice of any two dishes from a list of fifteen or twenty, is 1 rouble.

Dinners can be had for—

1 rouble 25 kopeks (6 courses) or
2 roubles 25   "   (8 courses)

The restaurants are generally open till about 2 A.M.

The numerous waiters are dressed in white on week days, on Sundays and feast days in coloured silk Tartar dresses. A large orchestrion plays from time to time during meals.

This restaurant has three head *chefs* and thirty-eight *chefs*, besides *pâtissiers* and all the smaller fry of the kitchen. The store-rooms for game, etc., form one of the sights of Moscow, and should be seen. There is a service of Sèvres china, which is very beautiful, and on which dinners are served on very special occasions. An extra charge, and a high one, is made for the use of this.

The Ermitage is unlike any other restaurant in the world in many respects. There is an admirable cellar of wines, and it is not a place for a man to give a big dinner at unless he is prepared to encounter a very big bill.

In Russia there is, as you will see by the subjoined menu of a typical Ermitage dinner, a sort of intermediate course between the soup and the fish called *petits pâtés*, which rather takes the place of an entrée, and although counted as nothing when it is preceded by the *Sakouska* (*i.e.* a preliminary "stand up" snack which waylays you at a separate buffet as you walk into dinner and consists of all sorts of *appétissants* such as caviar, cunningly smoked fish, olives, etc., with Kümmel and other liqueurs as an accompaniment) the smallest dinner resolves itself into a formidable repast that perhaps only a Russian would be capable of doing full justice to.

Ermitage Restaurant.

Menu.

Consommé Bariatinsky.
Petits Pâtés.
Timbale Napolitaine.

Vol-au-vent Rossini.
Friands à la Reine.
Tartelettes St-Hubert.
Esturgeon en Vin de Champagne.
Selle de Mouton d'Ecosse Nesselrode. Punch
Imperial.
Bécasses.
Cailles.
Salade et Concombres Salés.
Chouxfleurs. Sauce Polonaise.
Bombe en Surprise.
Dessert.

The Bolskoi Moscovski is opposite the town hall and has a spacious and fine central dining-hall. Here also the waiters are dressed in white, and an orchestrion discourses music during meal times. Its prices are practically the same as at the Ermitage.

Testoff's is another good restaurant where purely Russian dishes are served; it is therefore interesting and worth a visit, and gives a very good insight as to the national cuisine.

These restaurants are much frequented at lunch time, especially in summer, when families are out in Datchas or villas in the environs of Moscow, and the men have to lunch in town. In winter they are full until late in the evening.

One of the best lunch-places in Moscow is the Slaviansky Bazaar in Nikolski Street, Kitaigorod, situated in the city or business centre of Moscow. It is a mid-day resort of the business men and travellers staying at the hotel, but is more or less deserted afterwards. It has a spacious and lofty restaurant hall and takes in the *Times* and English illustrated papers. It was formerly noted for its regular English table for members of the colony, who, however, subsequently deserted it to some extent for the three main restaurants.

Here luncheons can be had with excellent choice *à la carte*. Dinners cost from 1 rouble 25 kopeks.

In addition to these regular restaurants there are several summer garden resorts of a gayer character with cafés, theatres, open-air stages, and various café-chantant amusements. These resorts are at their gayest in the early hours of the morning, till 4 A.M., when the company becomes somewhat varied, and as the guide-books sagely remark, "Gentlemen had better leave their ladies at the hotel."

These places are prettily laid out, and in the afternoon and early part of the evening serve to pass a pleasant hour or two in the summer. Dress clothes are not generally worn when visiting them.

In the town the two best ones are the Aquarium and the Ermitage Sad (Sad is Russian for garden), not the same as the Ermitage Restaurant above mentioned. Admission to gardens, 50 kopeks.

The Yar and the Strelna are favourite restaurant late-evening resorts near the Petrovski Park, a short drive out. The Yar is open in the summer and winter, but the Strelna in the winter only.

St. Petersburg

St. Petersburg has nominally three first-class restaurants, viz., the Bear (L'Ours) on the Bolschaya Kononschaya; the Restaurant de Paris, known as Cubat's, on the Bolschaya Marskaya; and Donon's on the Moika Canal. All of them are good. Donon's has an excellent cellar and supplies a good dinner if ordered in advance. The price of the set meals is very reasonable, about 2 roubles or 4s. 4d. per head; but the profits are made on the wines, which are ridiculously expensive (owing to the enormous duties). For instance, a bottle of *vin ordinaire* costs 4 roubles 50 kopeks, or 9s. 8d., and no bottle of dry champagne can be had for less than 10 roubles or 21s. 8d.; a whisky and soda is charged 1 rouble 50 kopeks, and in some places 2 roubles; a half bottle of wine is always charged 50 kopeks more than the actual half bottle price.

The Hôtel de France has a luncheon at 75 kopeks, or 1s. 6d., which is very popular with the business community of St. Petersburg, and it is crowded from 12.30 to 2 o'clock. The food is not high class but of a good bourgeois description, and the place is kept by a Belgian named Renault. It is one of the best hotels in St. Petersburg, and its situation is suited to the purpose; but, as a matter of fact, there is absolutely no first-class hotel either in St. Petersburg or Moscow, and sanitation is a factor that has not yet penetrated into the Russian intellect. A man who eats oysters in Russia, eats his own damnation, and at a high price in both senses; they are both costly and poisonous in a town where typhoid is easily contracted.

In the summer there are two good restaurants on the islands, a few miles from St. Petersburg, a sort of Richmond to St. Petersburg,—Felicien's, a dependence of Cubat's; and Ernest's, a branch of the Café de l'Ours, and managed by a brother of the proprietor. Both these have an excellent cuisine and cellar, but the charges, especially at Felicien's, are fairly extravagant. Bands of music and pretty gardens are features of these restaurants, and Felicien's has a terrace on the river opposite the Emperor's summer palace on the Island of Iliargin. They are both practically closed during the winter, excepting by arrangement or when sleighing parties make a rendezvous there.

There is also a German restaurant, Lemner's, at No. 18 Newsky Prospect, where a good, cheap German repast can be procured for 1 rouble and drink therewith, Russian pilsener or Munich beer.

Odessa

At the great port on the Black Sea the restaurant of the Hôtel de Londres Yastchouk is one of the best in Russia. Yastchouk was the name of its late proprietor, who died in 1902, and was a real lover of good cookery, enjoying nothing more than to serve an exquisite meal to a real connoisseur. When any gourmet came to his restaurant, he would ask him whether he came from the north or the south. If from the north, he would suggest a real southern meal, with *Rougets à la Grec* and the delicious *Agneau de lait*, unobtainable in St. Petersburg, and a ragout of *aubergines* and tomatoes. If from the south, he would recommend a good *Bortch* with *petits pâtés*, or a slice of *Koulebiaka*, a great pot-pie full of all kinds of good things, or some milk-white sucking-pig covered with cream and horse-radish. Yastchouk has joined the majority, but his restaurant is carried on in the same spirit as when he was alive.

Warsaw

Brühl's used to be the one good restaurant in the capital of Poland, but the restaurant of the Bristol, new, clean, smart, and cheap, with a French *maître-d'hôtel* in command, is commended and recommended. When the Bristol restaurant at night has all its electric lights in full glow it looks like the magic cave into which Aladdin penetrated.

CHAPTER XV

TURKEY

Turkish dishes—Constantinople restaurants.

Constantinople

One of the hotels in the restaurant at which very good food is obtainable is the Pera Palace; but the hundreds of dogs that are allowed to infest the city for scavenging purposes, and who disgracefully neglect their business in order to bark and howl dismally all night, would ruin the best hotel in creation. Therefore, if in the summer, I should advise any man to go to the Summer Palace Hotel at Therapia, a few miles from the city, on the Bosphorus, which is perfectly delightful, and to run into Constantinople by river steamer to visit the mosques, bazaars, etc.—but this by the way.

The best restaurant in Constantinople is Tokatlian's, in the Rue de Pera; it is very good but expensive, for all wines, spirits, etc., coming into Turkey have to pay a heavy duty. There is a strong native wine of a sauterne character made in Turkey, also Duzico, a sort of Kümmel liqueur, not bad, and Mastic, another *chasse*, especially nasty. You can obtain Turkish dishes at Tokatlian's. The Turkish *kahabs* and *pilaffs* of chicken are good, but their appearance is not appetising and they are too satisfying. A little rice and beef, rather aromatic in taste, is wrapped round with a thin vine leaf, in balls the size of a walnut, and eaten either hot or cold. This is called *Yalandji Dolmas*. *Yaourt* or *Lait Caillé* is a milk curd, rather like what is called *Dicke Milch* in Germany. *Aubergines* are eaten in every form; one method of cooking them, and that one not easily forgotten, is to smother a cold *aubergine* in onion, garlic, salt, and oil; this is named *Ymam Bayldi*. *Keinfté* are small meatballs tasting strongly of onions. Plaki fish, eaten cold; Picti fish in aspic; small octopi stewed in oil; *Moussaka*, vegetable marrows sliced, with chopped meat between the slices and baked; *Yachni*, meat stewed with celery and other vegetables; *Kebap*, "kabobs" with a bay-leaf between each little bit of meat; *Kastanato*, roasted chestnuts stewed in honey, and quinces treated in the same manner; vermicelli stewed in honey; and preserves of rose leaves, orange flowers, and jessamine, all are to be found in the Turkish cuisine. The *Rôti Kouzoum* is lamb impaled whole on a spit like a sucking-pig, which it rather resembles in size, being very small. It is well over-roasted and sent up whole. I am informed on the best authority that when a host wishes to do you honour he tears pieces off it with his fingers and places them before you, and you have to devour them in the same manner.

When I was in Turkey last year I had the misfortune not to be introduced to the privacy of a Turkish family gathering, so I have to confess that I have not yet accomplished this feat myself.

There is a very good fish when in season in the summer, called *espadon*, or sword-fish, but the butcher's meat, unless you have good teeth, is not often eatable. The natives are mostly vegetarians; beans, small cucumbers, rice and what cheap fruits may be in season are their principal food; water, about which they are most particular, is the principal beverage of all Turks from the highest to the lowest class.

I herewith give a typical Turkish dinner:—

Duzico.
Hors-d'œuvre.
Yalandji Dolmas.

POTAGE.

Crème d'Orge.

POISSON.

Espadon. Sce. Anchois.

ENTRÉE.

Boughou Kebabs.
Carni Yanik.

RÔTI.

Kouzoum.

LÉGUMES.

Bahmieh à l'Orientale.
Ymam Bayldi.

ENTREMETS.

Yaourt et Fruits.

The charges in Turkey on the whole are moderate, but the Turkish coinage is somewhat confusing, and even a Scotch Jew, who had been brought up in New York, would find it a matter of difficulty to hold his own with the unspeakable Turk when it came to a question of small change.

Tokatlian has a branch establishment of a bourgeois description for business people just outside the big bazaar at Stamboul, the Restaurant Grand Bazaar, where there are plenty of good dishes, besides native experiments, which are worth trying. Here the charges are very moderate.

The food at the Royal and Bellevue Hotels and Dimitri's is also good, and for supper you can go to Yani's, which is open practically all night, but perhaps not so eminently respectable as the other restaurants I have mentioned.

A.B.

CHAPTER XVI

GREECE

Grecian Dishes—Athens.

No one lives better than a well-to-do Greek outside his own country, and when he is in Greece his cook manages to do a great deal with comparatively slight material. A Greek cook can make a skewered pigeon quite palatable, and the number of ways he has of cooking quails, from the simple method of roasting them cased in bay leaves to all kinds of mysterious bakings after they have been soused in oil, are innumerable. There are *pillaus* without number in the Greek cuisine, chiefly of lamb, and it is safe to take for granted that anything *à la Grec* is likely to be something savoury, with a good deal of oil, a suspicion of onion, a flavour of parsley, and a good deal of rice with it. These, however, are some of the most distinctive dishes:—*Coucouretzi*, the entrails and liver of lamb, roasted on a spit; *Bligouri*, wheat coarsely ground, cooked in broth, and eaten with grated cheese; *Argokalamara*, a paste of flour and yolk of egg fried in butter with honey poured over it. All Greek cooking, as all Turkish is, should be done very slowly over a charcoal fire. A too great use of oil is the besetting sin of the indifferent Greek cook. The egg-plant is treated in half-a-dozen ways by the Greeks, stuffing them with some simple forced meat being the most common.

The food of the peasant is grain, rice, goat when he can get it, a skinny fowl as a great delicacy, milk, and strong cheese. A bunch of grapes and a piece of sour bread forms a feast for him.

The Grecian wines are not unpalatable but very light. They are mostly exported to Vienna, being fortified previous to their departure to enable them to stand the voyage, and again manipulated on their arrival, so that their original characteristics are considerably obliterated.

ATHENS

My trusted *collaborateur* A.B. went on a yachting tour in Grecian waters last spring, having a special intention of studying Greek restaurants. He wrote to me as to Athens, and his report was short and to the point: "Outside the hotels there is but one café, Solon's, principally used as a political rendezvous. Its attractions are of the most meagre description." A most grave *littérateur* to whom, as he had been lately travelling in Greece, and as I had not been there for ten years, I applied for supplementary information, applied the adjective "beastly" to all Greek restaurants, and added that the one great crying need of Greece and Athens is an American bar for the sale of cooling drinks in the Parthenon.

N.N.-D.

CPSIA information can be obtained
at www.ICGtesting.com
Printed in the USA
LVHW081251100520
655301LV00018B/769